St. Louis Community College

Forest Park
Florissant Valley
Meramec

Instructional Resources
St. Louis, Missouri

Inuit Women Artists

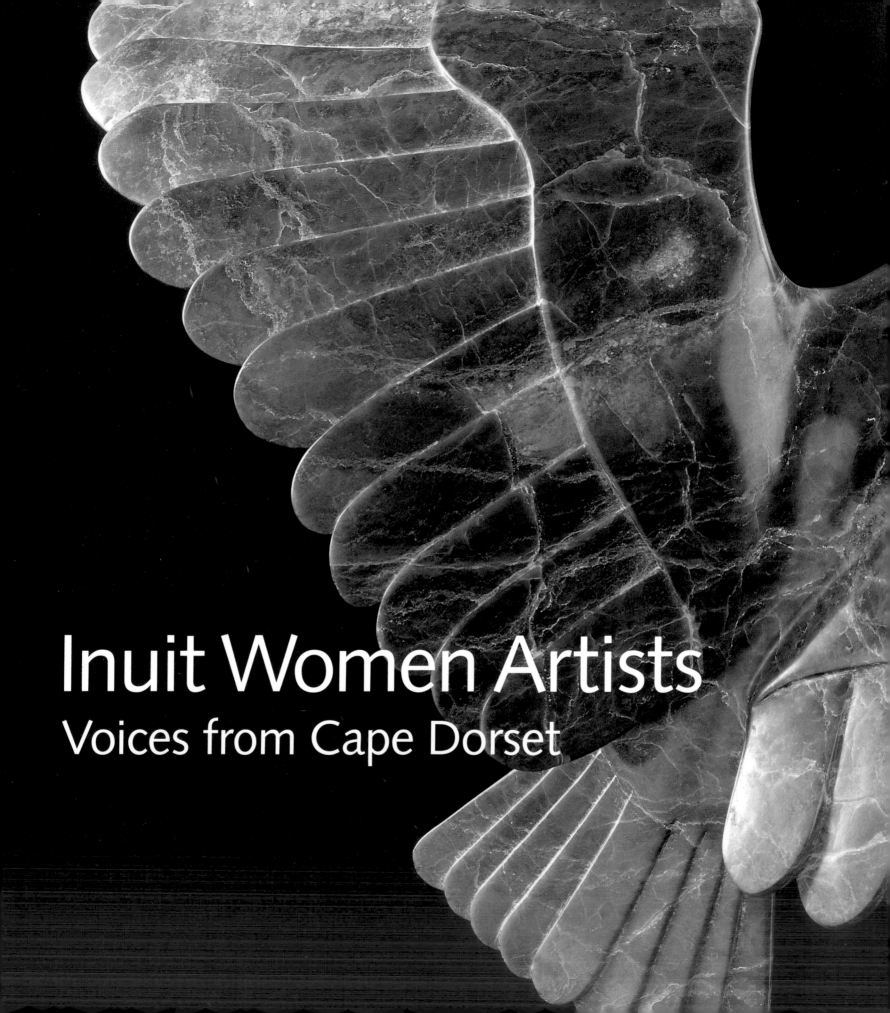

Inuit Women Artists
Voices from Cape Dorset

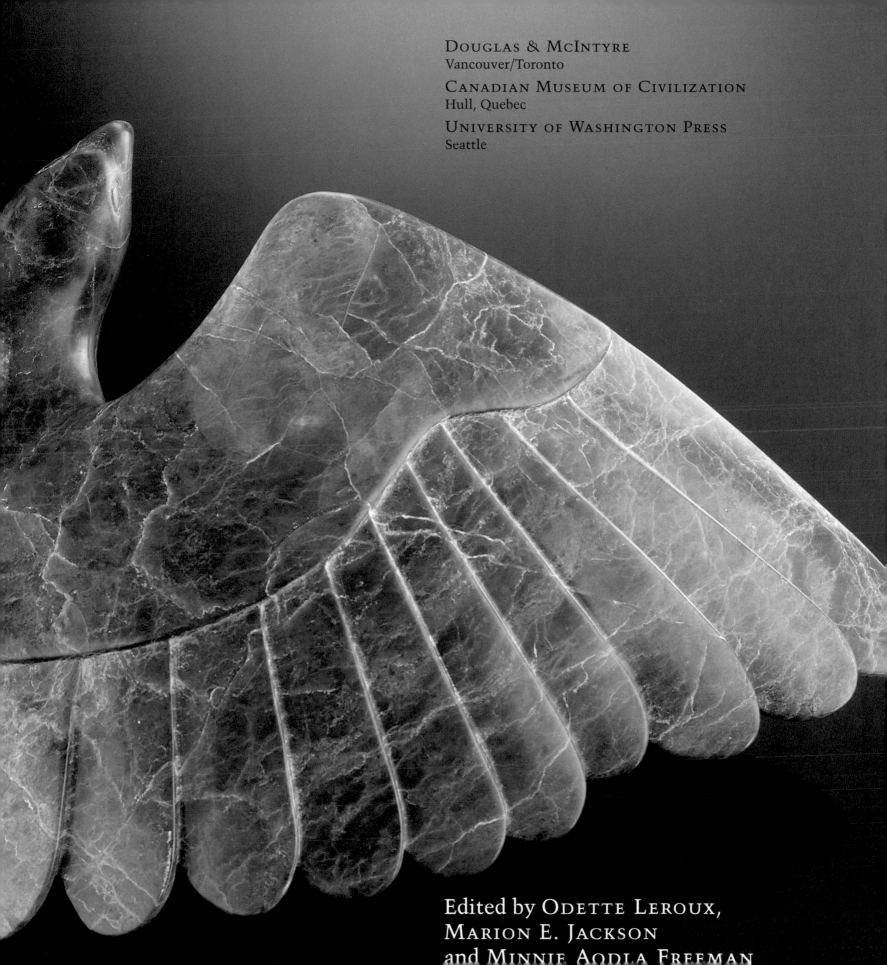

DOUGLAS & McINTYRE
Vancouver/Toronto

CANADIAN MUSEUM OF CIVILIZATION
Hull, Quebec

UNIVERSITY OF WASHINGTON PRESS
Seattle

Edited by ODETTE LEROUX,
MARION E. JACKSON
and MINNIE AODLA FREEMAN

Cet ouvrage a été publié simultanément en
français sous le titre *Femmes artistes inuit: Échos
de Cape Dorset*

Douglas & McIntyre
1615 Venables Street
Vancouver, British Columbia
V5L 2H1

Published simultaneously in the United States of
America by University of Washington Press,
P.O. Box 50096, Seattle, Washington 98145-5096

Canadian Cataloguing in Publication Data

Main entry under title:

Inuit women artists

ISBN 1-55054-131-5

1. Inuit—Northwest Territories—Cape Dorset—
Art. 2. Inuit women—Northwest Territories—
Cape Dorset. I. Leroux, Odette, 1942-. II. Freeman,
Minnie Aodla. III. Jackson, Marion E. (Marion
Elizabeth). IV. Canadian Museum of Civilization.
N6549.5.A54158 1994   704'.03971   C94-910241-5

Library of Congress Cataloging-in-Publication Data

Inuit women artists : voices from Cape Dorset /
    edited by Odette Leroux, Marion E. Jackson, and
    Minnie Aodla Freeman.
        p. cm.
    Includes bibliographical references.
    ISBN 0-295-97389-7 (Univ. of Wash. Press :
    acid-free paper)
    1. Inuit artists—Northwest Territories—Cape
Dorset. 2. Inuit women—Northwest
Territories—Cape Dorset. 3. Inuit—Northwest
Territories—Cape Dorset—Social life and cus-
toms. I. Leroux, Odette, 1942-   . II. Jackson,
Marion E. (Marion Elizabeth) III. Freeman,
Minnie Aodla. IV. Canadian Museum of
Civilization.
E99.E71565   1994
704'.042'097195--dc20   94-11711
                                          CIP

Front cover:
Napachie Pootoogook, 1938–
MY NEW ACCORDION
1989 lithograph, WBEC proof I/V

Back cover:
Oopik Pitsiulak, 1946–
OOPIK THINKING (back view)
1990 dark green stone, glass beads and wool cord
12.7 x 11.5 x 6.4 cm

Title page:
Ovilu Tunnillie, 1949–
HAWK TAKING OFF (detail)
circa 1987 green stone 17.4 x 72 x 38 cm

Photographs of the works of art by Harry Foster.
Photographs of the artists by Jimmy Manning,
except on pages indicated:
Norman E. Hallendy 45
Tessa Macintosh 73

Excerpts from *Pitseolak: Pictures out of My Life* by
Dorothy Harley Eber, © 1971, appear with permis-
sion of the author.
Excerpts from the 1978 and 1979 Cape Dorset
Print Catalogues appear with permission of the
West Baffin Eskimo Co-operative.

Editing by Margaret Campbell
Book design by George Vaitkunas
French translation by Christian Bérubé
Publication coordination by Cathrine Wanczycki
Printed and bound in Hong Kong by
C&C Offset Printing Co. Ltd.
Printed on acid-free paper ∞
Typefaces: Trump and Syntax

Contents

7 Foreword
   Dr. George F. MacDonald

8 Acknowledgements
10 Glossary
11 Explanatory Notes
12 Map

14 Introduction
   Minnie Aodla Freeman.

18 *Isumavut*
   The Artistic Expression of Nine Cape Dorset Women
   Odette Leroux

37 The Voices of Inuit Women
   Marion E. Jackson

43 Pitseolak Ashoona

71 Lucy Qinnuayuak

93 Kenojuak Ashevak

113 Qaunak Mikkigak

133 Napachie Pootoogook

159 Pitaloosie Saila

189 Oopik Pitsiulak

197 Mayoreak Ashoona

221 Ovilu Tunnillie

240 Good Memories
   Ann Meekitjuk Hanson

244 My Career Experiences
   Annie Manning

248 Traditional and Contemporary Roles of Inuit Women
   Minnie Aodla Freeman

251 Bibliography

Foreword

I AM DELIGHTED to introduce *Inuit Women Artists*. Unique in several ways, this project became possible with the agreement of the living artists: Kenojuak Ashevak, Qaunak Mikkigak, Napachie Pootoogook, Pitaloosie Saila, Oopik Pitsiulak, Mayoreak Ashoona and Ovilu Tunnillie, who have kindly agreed to write and share some of their intimate memories. The artists also generously agreed to be interviewed, to talk about their ideas and their art, and to provide titles for their sculptures. The meetings to discuss the works of art selected for this book became an occasion for them to share their artistic interests with one another.

Minnie Aodla Freeman played a major role in this endeavour. She encouraged their writing and facilitated the discussions. Her commitment and dedication to the project stimulated everyone in a very positive way. She became the artists' representative, wrote the introduction from an Inuit perspective, and edited all the texts in Inuktitut. At the same time, Minnie Freeman, Ann Meekitjuk Hanson, and Annie Manning wrote essays that reveal and illuminate the thoughts and accomplishments of modern Inuit women within their rich culture and traditions.

An advisory committee composed of Jimmy Manning, Assistant Manager, and Terrence P. Ryan, General Manager, West Baffin Eskimo Co-operative; Dorothy Harley Eber, writer; and Dr. Marion E. Jackson was of great assistance.

Jimmy Manning was the official photographer for the project in Cape Dorset. By his dedication, he captured the essence of the personality of each artist in a natural and individualistic way. His competence and personal relationship with the artists is reflected in his work.

The exhibition and the publication were initiated, conceived and curated by Odette Leroux, Curator of Inuit Art, and realized in close consultation and collaboration with Dr. Marion E. Jackson, Associate Professor of Art History, Carleton University. Dr. Jackson edited the English version of the artists' essays, wrote their biographies and introduced their texts. We are also indebted to Dr. Andrea Laforet, Chief, Canadian Ethnology Service; Dalma French, Exhibition Designer; Harry Foster, Photographer; Pierre Schnubb, Exhibition Project Manager; Jean-François Blanchette, Cathrine Wanczycki, Madeleine Choquette, Valencia Léger and Catherine Cunningham-Huston of the Publishing Division, for their support.

Thanks are also due to the following talented individuals: Margaret Campbell, editor of the English edition; book designer George Vaitkunas; and Christian Bérubé who produced the French language translation.

I would like to express our sincere appreciation to the Inuit artists and all other contributors as well as the lenders, the Inuktitut translators, and others who kindly provided assistance in various ways.

Inuit Women Artists brings a new perspective on Inuit art and opens the door for a new development in the exchange between Inuit artists and writers, Inuit art enthusiasts, and our public audience.

Dr. George F. MacDonald
Executive Director
Canadian Museum of Civilization

---

facing page:
Oopik Pitsiulak, 1946–
OOPIK THINKING
1990

dark green stone, glass
beads and wool cord
12.7 X 11.5 X 6.4 cm
unsigned

Acknowledgements

The artists:
Kenojuak Ashevak
Mayoreak Ashoona
Pitseolak Ashoona
Qaunak Mikkigak
Oopik Pitsiulak
Napachie Pootoogook
Lucy Qinnuayuak
Pitaloosie Saila
Ovilu Tunnillie

The contributors:
Minnie Aodla Freeman
Marion E. Jackson
Odette Leroux
Annie Manning
Ann M. Meekitjuk Hanson

The advisors:
Dorothy Harley Eber, Marion E. Jackson,
Jimmy Manning, Terrence P. Ryan

Communicators/Interpreters/Translators:
In Cape Dorset:
Ooloosie Ashevak
Mark Pitseolak
Josie Pootoogook
Meakie Pudlat
Sana Pudlat
Kataoga Saila
Ningiokulu Teevee

In Ottawa:
Susan Aglukark
Nipisha Bracken
Leah d'Idlout-Paulson
Deborah Evaluarjuk
Sadie Hill
Bernadette Immaroitok
Leonie Kunnuk
Jeannie Manning
Katolic Utatnaq
Rachel Qitsualik

In Yellowknife:
Elizabeth Qulaut

Interviews:
Sana Pudlat
Tikitu Qinnuayuak

West Baffin Eskimo Co-operative:
Mr. Qabavoak Qatsiya, President
Terrence P. Ryan, General Manager
Jimmy Manning, Assistant Manager &
   Photographer
Joemie Takpaujai, Assistant
Leslie Boyd, Project Manager
Janet Mayheu, Office Manager
Margaret Gillis, Administrator
John Westren, Showroom & Sales Manager

Hamlet Office, Cape Dorset, Northwest Territories:
Chuck Gilhuly, Senior Administrative Officer

Peter Pitseolak School:
Jerry Huculak, Douglas Workman, Terry Young
   Principals in 1991, 1992, 1993–94
Oqutaq Mikkigak, Janitor

Economic Development and Tourism:
Government of the Northwest Territories
Robert Jaffray, Cape Dorset

Science Institute of the Northwest Territories,
Yellowknife

Translation:
Secretary of State Canada,
Romance and General Multilingual Section:
Peter Christensen & Patrick McNamer

Nortex:
David Roberts
Michael Roberts

Indian and Northern Affairs Canada,
Inuit Art Section:
Maria Muehlen, Ingo Hessel, Jeanne L'Espérance,
Lori Cutler, Patrick Adams

Individuals:
Eugene Arima
Sandra B. Barz
Wallace Brannen
Dorothy Harley Eber
Quintin J. Finlay
Norman N. Hallendy
Margaret P. Hess
Alma Houston
James A. Houston

H. J. Jones
Mary Simpson
Dorothy Speak
George Swinton
William E. Taylor, Jr.
David Webster
Nigel Wilford

Art Galleries & Museums:
Dennis Cardiff & Darcy Morey, Art Bank, The
   Canada Council, Ottawa, Ontario
Virginia Watt, Canadian Guild of Crafts Quebec,
   Montréal, Quebec
Lorraine Brandson, Eskimo Museum, Churchill,
   Manitoba
Patricia Ainsley, Glenbow Museum, Calgary,
   Alberta
Ollie Ittinuar, Inuit Cultural Institute, Rankin
   Inlet, Northwest Territories
Demetra Christales, Laurentian University
   Museum and Arts Centre, Sudbury, Ontario
Jean Blodgett, McMichael Canadian Art
   Collection, Kleinburg, Ontario
Bruce Grenville, Mendel Art Gallery, Saskatoon,
   Saskatchewan
Rosa Ho, Museum of Anthropology, University of
   British Columbia, Vancouver, British Columbia
Marie Routledge, National Gallery of Canada,
   Ottawa, Ontario
Denise Bekkema, Nunatta Sunaqutangit Museum,
   Iqaluit, Northwest Territories
Norman Zepp & Cynthia Waye Cook, Ontario Art
   Gallery, Toronto, Ontario
Joanne Bird, Prince of Wales Northern Heritage
   Centre, Yellowknife, Northwest Territories
Patricia M. Feheley, Toronto Dominion Bank,
   Toronto, Ontario
Jeffrey Spalding & Lucie Linhart, University of
   Lethbridge Art Gallery, Lethbridge, Alberta
Helle Viirlaid, Vancouver Art Gallery, Vancouver,
   British Columbia
Terrence P. Ryan & Leslie Boyd, West Baffin
   Eskimo Co-operative, Cape Dorset, Northwest
   Territories & Toronto, Ontario
Darlene Wight, Winnipeg Art Gallery, Winnipeg,
   Manitoba

Commercial Galleries:
Barbara McCaffery, Canada House, Banff, Alberta
Patricia M. Feheley, Feheley Fine Arts Inc.,
  Toronto, Ontario
Raymond Brousseau, Galerie aux multiples collec-
  tions, Québec, Quebec
Mark London, Galerie Elca London, Montréal,
  Quebec
Erla Arbuckle, Gallery Indigena, Waterloo, Ontario
Phillip Gevik, Gallery Phillip, Toronto, Ontario
Alma Houston, Houston North Gallery,
  Lunenburg, Nova Scotia
John Bohm, Igloo-Art, Montréal, Quebec
Harold Seidelman, Images Art Gallery, Toronto,
  Ontario
Joseph Antonitsch, Inuit Galerie, Mannheim, West
  Germany
Joseph Murphy, Inuit Gallery of Vancouver,
  Vancouver, British Columbia
Tom and Helen Webster, Iqaluit Fine Arts Studio
  Limited, Iqaluit, Northwest Territories
Claude Baud, L'iglou art esquimau, Douai, France
Leon Lippel, Lippel Gallery Inc., Montréal, Quebec
Judith Kardosh, Marion Scott Ltd., Vancouver,
  British Columbia
Ann Jenkins & Howard Isaacs, The Innuit Gallery,
  London, Ontario
John Bell & Ruby Brownstone, The Isaacs/Innuit
  Gallery, Toronto, Ontario
Faye Settler, The Upstairs Gallery, Winnipeg,
  Manitoba

Lenders:
Art Bank, The Canada Council, Ottawa, Ontario
Canadian Guild of Crafts Quebec, Montréal,
  Quebec
Houston North Gallery, Lunenburg, Nova Scotia
Images Art Gallery, Toronto, Ontario
Inuit Cultural Institute, Rankin Inlet, Northwest
  Territories/Prince of Wales Northern Heritage
  Centre, Yellowknife, Northwest Territories
National Gallery of Canada, Ottawa, Ontario
Ontario Art Gallery, Toronto, Ontario
West Baffin Eskimo Co-operative, Cape Dorset,
  Northwest Territories
A private collector who wishes to remain
  anonymous

Collectors:
Dr. and Mrs. Albert Yuzpe, London, Ontario
General Electric Canada, Mississauga, Ontario
West Baffin Eskimo Co-operative & McMichael
  Canadian Art Collection

Volunteers:
Mychelle Gay, Lucienne Gratton Sincennes,
Heather E. McLean, Angela R. Skinner

Canadian Museum of Civilization Staff:

For the exhibition:
Odette Leroux, Curator of Inuit Art
Dalma French, Exhibition Designer
Harry Foster, Photographer
Pierre Schnubb, Exhibition Project Manager
Valérie Pinard, Exhibitions Clerk
Pamela Brooks, School Programme Coordinator
Margery Toner, Photo Archivist
Marjorie Stanton, Loan Officer
Kitty Bishop-Glover, Senior Registrar
Marilyn Boyd, Registrar
Margot Reid, Cataloguer
Jim Donnelly, Head Collections Reserves
Kelly Cameron, Collections Preparator
Steve Racine, Fabrication & Installation

Conservation Division:
Tom Govier, Manager
Charles Hett, David Theobald, Sylvia Kindl,
John Kohler, Paul Lauzon, John Moses

Publishing Division:
Jean François-Blanchette, Chief
Cathrine Wanczycki, Madeleine Choquette,
Valencia Léger, Dominique Fortier, Paula Sousa,
Gilles Dansereau, and Catherine Cunningham-
Huston

Canadian Ethnology Service:
Andrea Laforet, Chief
J. Garth Taylor, Curator of Arctic Ethnology
Pamela Coulas, Programmes Administrator
Fatima Tigmi, Secretary

*We wish to express our most sincere gratitude to
all of those too numerous to mention who kindly
provided us with their collaboration and assistance with this project.*

Odette Leroux,
Marion E. Jackson,
Minnie Aodla Freeman

Glossary

ajagak	Inuit version of the ring-and-pin game
amaut	carrying pouch on the back of a woman's parka
amauti	woman's parka
amautiit	plural of *amauti*
amaruq	wolf
amaruuk	two wolves
amaruit	more than two wolves
Arnakutaaq	"tall woman"; name given to Alma Houston
atigi	inner parka
avataq	inflated sealskin float
igloo	(illu) house made of snow blocks
inniutik	drying rack
Inuit	the people
Inuk	one person, human; singular of Inuit
Inuuk	two persons, humans
inukshuk	(inussuk) cairn built of rocks; may be in the shape of a human
Inuktitut	(Inuttitut) the Inuit language
Isumavut	our thoughts
kajjarnartuq	beautiful scenery
kamik	one boot
kamiik	two or two pairs of boots
kamiit	more than two pairs of boots
kinngait	mountains
kiputiit	natural causeway under the water that is used to walk between the mainland and an island
kuanniq	edible seaweed
nanuk	bear
natturaq	ivory clasp
Nunavut	our land
pauttuutit	drying stakes (also the name chosen for the Inuit Women's Association, based in Ottawa)
pilartutuk	skinning the seal (title on print, page 90: *Pilatuktu*)

qajaq	one kayak
qajaak	two kayaks
qajait	more than two kayaks
qallunaat	white people
qarmaq	stone house, sod house, tent-like hut
qaumutik	sled
qulliq	traditional oil lamp made of stone
qulliik	two oil lamps
qulliit	more than two oil lamps
qurvik	toilet bowl
Saumik	"left-handed one"; name given to James Houston
Taleelayu	(Talilaju) sea goddess, Sedna, mermaid
Tausunni	Inuit program
timiarjuaat	large birds (title on print, page 94: *Timiatjuak*)
Tiuli	name given to Terrence Ryan, General Manager and Artistic Advisor of the West Baffin Eskimo Co-operative
titirtugait	printmaking
tulukaraq	young raven (title on print, page 89: *Tulukara*)
tusarautiniq	term referring to how we speak to each other
tuurngaq	spirit
ujjuk	bearded seal
ujjuuk	two bearded seals
ujjuit	more than two bearded seals
uppaaraq	one young snowy owl
uppik	one snowy owl
uppiik	two snowy owls
uppiit	more than two snowy owls
ulu	woman's knife
uluuk	two woman's knives
uluit	more than two woman's knives
umiaq	sealskin boat (title on drawing, page 78: *Umiak*)
uujuq	stew

Explanatory Notes

In this book, the artists are presented chronologically from the eldest to the youngest. This approach provides a clear picture of the evolution of the art of women from Cape Dorset.

Today, most Inuit people have a surname but these women were known by their traditional first name. In order to follow the tradition, they are often referred to here using their most common name.

Measurements are in centimeters. Height precedes width for the works on paper whereas height, width, and depth are the dimensions for the sculptures.

The year a work was created is shown immediately following its title. When the catalogue year differs from the year of creation, the abbreviation *cat.* indicates this, as in *(1982, cat. 1983)*. In the Leroux essay, *Isumavut*, the abbreviation *fig.* followed by a number refers to an illustration of the work found within the essay, as in *(1967, fig. 6)*. References in this essay to illustrations that appear in the rest of the book include page numbers to enable the reader to refer to each piece of art, as in *My Dolls (1967, page 163)*.

Almost all sculptures were titled by the artists and a few prints were retitled by the authors in order to be more accurate. The quotes for the works of art are by the artists unless otherwise indicated. They were extracted from the Marion E. Jackson 1979 interviews, Odette Leroux 1991 interviews, Marion E. Jackson and Odette Leroux 1992 interviews and Dorothy Harley Eber's publication *Pitseolak: Pictures out of My Life.*

All the works of art are drawn from the collection of the Canadian Museum of Civilization unless otherwise indicated.

The photographs of the works of art are by Harry Foster and the photographs of artists are by Jimmy Manning unless otherwise indicated.

The works of art are reproduced by permission of the artists, through the West Baffin Eskimo Co-operative.

NORTHWEST TERRITORIES

ARCTIC CIRCLE

○ **Repulse Bay**

DISTRICT OF

KEEWATIN

SOUTHAMPTON
ISLAND

Coral Harbour
○

Baker Lake
○

COATS

ISLAND

Chesterfield Inlet
○

Rankin Inlet
○

HUDSON BAY

Arviat
○

Dewey Soper
Bird Sanctuary

Bowman Bay
Game Sanctuary

Amadjuak
Lake

BAFFIN ISLAND

○ Iqaluit

Frobisher
Bay

○ Nuvujuak

FOXE PENINSULA

○ Nurata

Kangia
Shapujuak ○ ○
Igalallik ○ ○ Ikirashaq
○ Ittiliakjuk
○ Shatureetuk
Kangisujuak ○ Keatuk
○ ● Cape Dorset
(Kinngait)

○ Qarmaajuk
(Amadjuak H.B.C. Post)

● Lake Harbour

SALISBURY

ISLAND

HUDSON STRAIT

NOTTINGHAM

ISLAND

○ Purtuniq

○ Kangiqsujuaq

Cap Wolstenholme

○ Salluit

Qikiqtarjuaq
Inlet (?) called
Anaulirvik

○
Ivujivik

MANSEL

ISLAND

(PUJJUNAQ)

Kuujjuaq ○

○ Akulivik

OTTAWA

ISLANDS

○ Povungnituk

QUEBEC

NUNAVIK

○ Inukjuak

Introduction

Minnie Aodla Freeman

I HAVE HAD THE PLEASURE of being involved with the famous Cape Dorset women artists. Although I am neither an artist nor famous, I was involved with these artists as an Inuit writer. In February 1991, I travelled from Edmonton to accompany Odette Leroux to Cape Dorset to spend twelve days with the artists.

Cape Dorset is situated on the southwest of Baffin Island in the Northwest Territories. At one time it was a main trading post where Inuit from the outlying camps came to trade at the Hudson's Bay Company store. Today, Cape Dorset is a growing settlement where traditional camping days are outnumbered by days spent in other trades. The population at the present is just over 1,000. Inuit call this place "Kinngait," meaning "the mountains." Mountains are everywhere. In fact, the community of Cape Dorset is nestled in two valleys, but as the population grows some of the houses are being built on the mountains.

February is not the best time of the year in Cape Dorset for those who are not accustomed to its weather. At this time, it is bitterly cold with the temperature almost all the time between -40° C and -60° C. The women artists were all born here or in the outlying camps. All the artists were brought up with traditional values, but their adaptation to modern society makes them remarkable. Why do I say, "makes them remarkable"? Because over the years that I have lived in southern Canada, I have not met any other culture that has adapted so suddenly to another, surviving all its shortcomings, its bad influences, and the misplaced good intentions of well-meaning people. Despite the sudden introduction of new ways, the Inuit women have remained the kind of people their traditional culture trained them to be: patient, polite, giving, and always pleasant to see, with smiles on their faces. The smile is one of the important gestures in Inuit culture; it can tell you everything about a person.

Some of these artists were trained to adapt to the modern world almost by accident. If they had been given a choice about coming to southern cities, I do not think they would have come. But some of the artists contracted tuberculosis during the 1950s and early 1960s. Their prolonged stays in southern hospitals made them adapt to the southern world. Some of them were very young and learned to speak the English language. The survival training they had received in their own culture helped them a great deal, enabling them to maintain their language and cultural values. Through their art, you can see that they value their culture deeply. It is not very easy to adapt from one culture to another unless one has a very deep interest in one's new environment. Over the years, I have seen Inuit trying to keep their culture while people from other cultures disregard their culture, their own foundations. Some do this to be accepted by their peers.

The artists have not been spoiled by their fame. They have had many chances to act spoiled. Yes, they are proud of what they have done. Some of them have travelled abroad for art shows and some have travelled all over Canada. Some of them have placed murals in big cities. But they do not pretend to be anything but themselves. They value their traditional culture. At the same time, they have a great deal of respect for the new culture that has been emerging in their community over the last fifty years.

One of these artists, Mayoreak Ashoona, lives on the land in an outpost camp. While in Cape Dorset, I was asked to visit that camp, but, to my deep regret, the weather would not co-operate. So I will try to describe the camp as best I can from the story Mayoreak told me.

It is a one-hour drive by skidoo from Cape Dorset. Her home is provided by the hamlet government and is heated by oil. Although it does not have all the conveniences of the houses in Cape Dorset, Mayoreak totally enjoys living there. She knows very well that her companion artists have all the conveniences, yet she chooses to live the traditional way. She says that her mind is always at rest and her psychological being is happy. The surroundings of her environment are always familiar. She also told me that her drawings derive from her surroundings at her camp. I understand her contentment very well.

Somehow I could not help comparing myself to her, although I doubt very much that I could fill her big shoes. I was born in traditional surroundings. I grew up eating Inuit food exclusively. I slept in camps from one season to another and harnessed and ran along side of dog teams. But today I have all the conveniences of the modern world: running water, electric lights, washing and dishwashing machines. I can drive a car whenever I want to go anywhere, and I have all kinds of choices for shopping. Here, I thought I was brave for having adapted!

We Inuit have adapted and adopted many different words to accommodate our understanding of our changing world. Very often we make up a word that may not exist in our language in order to express something from another culture. The word "art," for example, did not exist in Inuktitut. That is not to say that Inuit art did not exist, but it was a serious matter in the old days. Traditionally, Inuit made amulets, decorations for the body and for hunting equipment, and replicas of everyday objects to attach to their clothing. A lot of traditional art was made for burial purposes. Those objects were taken seriously. To *qallunaat*, some Inuit use of charms may not sound very serious. A lot of traditional art was used to "shoo away" bad spirits, to bring good luck when an event took place, to encourage a young person to bravery, and also to escort the dead to the good spirits rather than have their spirits floating around nowhere. Very often a charm would be made for a newborn child. Some charms were made to bond closer a very special relationship. Some of these uses are still common today, especially for the bonding of special relationships. It was only when *qallunaat* saw this traditional art that it became "art."

Today the word *titirtugait* is very fascinating to Inuit like me. It is the word being used for "printmaking." Inuit from Cape Dorset feel that it could be either a traditional or a modern word. They feel it was made up during the 1950s when printmaking was introduced and somebody tried to translate the word "stencil." They also believe that it is a word that died and then was revived. They say it was once used to describe the picture-message writing on skins and tusks. However, the significant thing is that all Inuit know what it means today.

To me, it is a word that will be debatable for years to come. It is like the word *qallunaat*. *Qallunaat* does not mean "white people"; it could mean either "people with beautiful eyebrows" or "people with beautiful manufactured material."

During our twelve days in Cape Dorset, the artists got to know Odette Leroux, the curator from the Canadian Museum of Civilization, and myself. Some of the artists already knew Odette from past art shows. They were so appreciative of the chance to talk face-to-face about themselves and not just about their work. Although they had already heard about this project from Jimmy Manning of the West Baffin Co-operative, when asked if they would like to write about their own thoughts, their mouths opened. Almost in unison, the word *daa* came out of their mouths. It is a very expressive word used by Inuit in surprise, disgust, delight, or total agitation. I do not know a *qallunaat* word that could match the word *daa* but comparable phrases might be "oh, my goodness," "good grief," "for heaven's sake," "good God, you must be mad!" or "do you mean it?" Some of the artists were in shock that they were being asked to write about themselves. They were amazed that after all these years somebody finally asked them to write their own words. All together they began to talk among themselves. One kept saying, "That is going to be fun." At that moment, I wished Odette could speak in Inuktitut instead of having to

depend on my translation of their delight. But I am sure the curator could see the expressions on their faces.

"What do you think?" the curator asked.

"We have never been asked to write about ourselves. We have always been written about."

When one of the artists finished that sentence, one could hear a pin drop.

Two women spoke their minds.

"What do we write about?"

The curator and I looked at each other. Then she turned to the artists and said, "Minnie will explain."

What was I to tell them? First, it was very odd for me to talk about writing to my fellow Inuit women. We are all from a strong oral culture, and here we were discussing writing. We have indeed changed and adapted a great deal. Second, as an Inuk brought up with very deep traditional values, I found it very hard to take the lead, especially as I have been raised never to speak out knowledgeably in front of elders. Some of the artists are my elders At that moment I had to forget my own thoughts. I had to think how to teach them—correctly and politely and without interference—to write. All of the artists knew how to write in Inuktitut, the syllabic system, but they were worried because they did not know how to write in English. I explained that that was no problem. They would write in their own way about their thoughts, their lives, their experiences, and especially about their own feelings about their own lives, their families and their professions.

It was fun! I cannot wait to see it all together and to hear the delight of the women when they see their handwritten work transformed by modern technology.

As in other changing cultures, Inuit now have a greater understanding of the possible professions that will be open to them in the future. While the children of these famous artists are studying for their future professions at school, the artists are holding together the very foundations of their culture through their art. Although some young Inuit may not realize it, the answer to their need to have an important identity is right under their noses in their parents' art. How many will take up art is not known. How many, if they take it up, will have the natural ability or the imagination? Some do not even realize that they are clothed and fed and able to have fun because of their parents' art.

In addition to the artists, two other women are involved in this publication. One, Annie Manning, is a former Justice of the Peace in Cape Dorset, the first Inuit woman to hold this post. The other, Ann Meekitjuk Hanson, was the first Inuit woman to become Deputy Commissioner of the Northwest Territories. Both have taken on great responsibility for the future of the Inuit—"responsibility" not in the sense that Inuit are not capable themselves but in the sense of giving our young Inuit the kinds of role models that they very much need to see today. They have undertaken to ensure that justice among Inuit will be fair, and that the government that runs and rules the lives of Inuit will care about the changes taking place among Inuit. Like a lot of Inuit women in our generation, both of these women had traditional upbringings. Yet they took on tasks alien to their culture, and they adapted to them. Both are building the trust necessary between two cultures that live side-by-side today. These two women also took time to write their own thoughts and experiences.

Because I watched and visited some of the artists in their private homes while they were drawing, I want to express my own private thoughts about their art. People should enjoy these artists deeply *now*, not wait until they have died or cannot draw any more. Both Inuit and *qallunaat* alike should speak of them more often and should talk about their names and works. As we look into the future, not many people will have seen all the traditional scenes that these women hold in their minds. In the next generation of women, how many will have seen a dog team? How many will have seen a man waiting at the seal hole on the ice for hours at -60° C? How many will have seen a snowy owl sitting on the peak of *kinngait*, wisely moving only its eyes? It is because these artists have seen and felt and lived these experiences that they are so good at their art. They have handled the equipment traditionally used for making the Inuit way of life comfortable. They carry in them the very survival techniques that have brought them to this day.

I hope stone carving and printmaking will never become a dying art. I hope the people who are put in charge of the West Baffin Eskimo Co-op will always care about the artists and the Co-op's relationship with the environment. That their working conditions are pleasant is what the Inuit people appreciate most. I hope the artists, future and present, will always have the trust that they have today with the people involved in the Co-op. I hope the present enthusiasm is passed on to artists who will come to the building in the future. It is a good feeling as an artist in a small community to get up and dress and walk to the Co-op to pick up more supplies. I hope artists of the future are presently being sought and encouraged to take up the art material readily available to them. I know that the traditional knowledge is slowly—very fast in some areas—being lost. Very often we forget or do not make efforts to find capable people to continue something when it is no longer making a lot of money. Very often Inuit have a lot of capabilities but no one to go to. I hope very much that this does not happen to the artists because when an artist dies, the art dies with them.

I know I learned a lot from all of these artists, and we made bonds in Inuit ways.

Isumavut
The Artistic Expression of Nine Cape Dorset Women

Odette Leroux

ART IS A RELATIVELY NEW MEDIUM of expression for Inuit women. It has evolved only since the 1960s, nurtured in various artists' workshops that have sprung up in scattered communities across the Arctic. Carving was a man's art and few women had ventured to experiment in that field. The introduction of graphics in the late 1950s in Cape Dorset, however, unleashed a wealth of latent talent. Women responded to the opportunity to work with this new medium, perhaps because it could be handled in the privacy of their home. Whatever the reasons, the results have been impressive. The art that these women have created leads the viewer into a world torn between the traditional and the modern, the mystical and the rational. But more than this, the art looks through female eyes, noticing colours, clothes, relationships with children, chores that demand daily attention, hardships that must be endured, customs that must be passed on, beauty that underlies even the bleakest landscape.

The art of Inuit women opens a unique window on a remote world. My long-standing fascination with this window was heightened in 1990 when I was asked to write a few short biographies on Inuit women artists for the *Encyclopedia of Twentieth Century North American Women Artists*. As I worked, I became enthralled by the themes I perceived in the art and I began to conceive of a project that would pull together the work of several artists. The enormous distances and daunting costs made it impractical to include women's art from across the Canadian Arctic, so I decided to focus on just one community of women artists: Cape Dorset.

It was in this community that the efforts of James Houston to encourage art among the Inuit people had its tentative beginnings in the early 1950s. Houston and his wife, Alma, lived in Cape Dorset for ten years, cultivating the rise of interest in the graphic arts and providing a nucleus around which an artistic community could coalesce. Their work has been continued by their successor, Terrence Ryan. In his position as General Manager and Artistic Advisor, Ryan's foresight and entrepreneurship has resulted in national and international recognition of the talents and creativity of Cape Dorset artists. Today, the West Baffin Eskimo Co-operative is the heart of the community, serving the artists as an archival centre, a source of supplies, and a marketing company. Several accomplished women artists live in or near Cape Dorset, nine of whom are represented here.

As Marion (Mame) Jackson had lived in Cape Dorset and had conducted interviews with several artists there in 1979, I asked if she would be interested in collaborating with me. She was delighted and agreed.

The idea of having the women write about themselves I owe to my memory of a 1975 exhibition held at the National Gallery of Canada entitled *Some Canadian Women Artists*, curated by Mayo Graham. Its catalogue included the artists' overviews of their style and comments on their personal concerns. With Mame's encouragement, I decided to develop this approach.

The adventure began in December 1990 when Jimmy Manning, an Inuit photographer and Assistant Manager at the West Baffin Co-operative, met with the artists to explain the project. Enthusiastically, the women agreed to participate, although many had never written before. Jimmy continued to assist us throughout the project and his help has been invaluable. He kept in touch with the artists, co-ordinated our field trips, and always provided me with the most accurate information.

In February 1991, Minnie Aodla Freeman travelled with me to Cape Dorset for a full discussion of the project in Inuktitut. To our surprise, Mayoreak Ashoona, Qaunak Mikkigak and Napachie Pootoogook brought their completed stories to our first meeting, while Kenojuak Ashevak, Pitaloosie Saila and Ovilu Tunnillie had started writing and told us they intended to finish before our departure.

We had taken with us a portfolio for each artist with colour photocopies of their works of art, including graphics, jewellery and sculptures gathered from museums, galleries and private collections. This was the first time any of the artists had seen their works gathered together in one collection and they were happy to pick a few of their favourite works and comment on them. These commentaries offered new insights into the artist's own perspective and appear here as captions to the works of art.

The artists enjoyed meeting together to discuss their ideas and their work. For many, this was their first opportunity to exchange opinions in a group discussion. They were excited to talk about their work in front of colleagues and to have the opinion of outsiders on the aesthetic value of their work and on their style. They told us later that the exchange had given them much encouragement to pursue their artistic careers. Some also shared stories about Pitseolak Ashoona and Lucy Qinnuayuak who are no longer living.

Our farewell dinner at Pitaloosie's house was a wonderful caribou stew prepared by Pitaloosie, three types of bannock, and desserts. After the meal, we had all kinds of entertainment, including accordion music (everyone had a try at it) as well as throat singing by Qaunak, Napachie and Minnie, Inuit folk music, and a video of Inuit square dancing and music. We also danced. Kenojuak Ashevak is a really good dancer. We left with fine memories of this evening at the Sailas' home and a sense of a strong bond of friendship.

In February 1992, I travelled to Cape Dorset once more with Marion Jackson to further interview each artist and verify details of the texts, the biographies and the statements about the art. The exceptional sculptures of Oopik Pitsiulak had been added to our project and during this visit Oopik recorded her life story and observations on tape, and this became the basis of her story.

With the end of this second meeting came an understanding that the project would have consequences we had not imagined. As Mayoreak Ashoona said, "Since you came last year I felt the need to write more about my way of life to be transmitted to my children and my grandchildren." She then gave us a new manuscript of her autobiography written in syllabics.

This compulsion to record what is passing is evident in the work of these artists. They are all aware that Inuit society is increasingly vulnerable to outside cultural influences. The arrival of mass communication has thrown their traditional society into a state of upheaval, and as a result, the perception, tastes and behaviour of the inhabitants of the North are changing rapidly. The artists mirror these changes in their work, but they are also concerned to capture the past and preserve what they remember and what they have experienced. We realised that we might have provided an unexpected extra impetus in this direction.

The project also made it imperative that major works from museums, galleries and private collectors in Canada and abroad be identified. Not only were the artists energized by seeing works that had been dispersed around the world gathered into portfolios, but approximately twenty-one sculptures were subsequently acquired for the National Inuit Art Collection. They are part of Canada's cultural heritage and will be available to be admired by future generations.

The stories, comments, sculptures, prints and drawings presented in this volume open the personal universe of the women artists of Cape Dorset. Before discussing their art in detail, however, I would like to introduce these women. Each one has her own highly individualistic style and her own distinct way of reproducing form, line, curve and angle, and of selecting graphic elements, dimensions, surfaces, textures and colours. George Swinton, in his book *Sculpture of the Inuit*, suggests that their inspiration is essentially based in realism. Certainly the narrative content of the art is often autobiographical or historical, and shows occasional flashes of humour and fantasy.

Pitseolak Ashoona

Pitseolak Ashoona works only in drawings and prints. Her drawings are more than occasionally autobiographical anecdotes, as Dorothy Harley Eber noted in her book *Pitseolak: Pictures out of My Life*. They constitute a true cultural legacy, the equivalent of an encyclopedia of a way of life. Through her pictorial work, Pitseolak Ashoona gives a fascinating and highly authentic documentation of her culture. Her vision and iconographic vocabulary remain unequalled.

Pitseolak began working in the 1960s. Initially, she concentrated on engraving; her production was astonishing, considering the technical demands of the medium. *Untitled* (1962, page 47) is a comparative study of the representation of three faces with very different contours. This exercise helped her define and master the execution of shapes. Another engraving, also called *Untitled* (1962, page 48), is notable for the boldness of the strokes and the play of lines in a manifestly experimental work. From 1963 on, Pitseolak's work shows her mastery of her technique. *Furry Owl* (1962, page 49) and *Witch and Friends* (1963, page 50) reveal a slightly whimsical touch to her creative vision. *Happy Family* (1963, page 48) and *People* (1964, page 52) provide invaluable information about the clothing and customs of her people. The artist's genius for dynamic composition can best be understood from a comparison of the faces of the characters in the 1962 study with the joyous expressions of those in *People*. *Woman and Dogs* (1967) and *Woman with Geese* (1966, cat. 1967), both of which appear on page 54, are typical of Pitseolak's drawings and her characteristic full-face and profile representations.

Towards the end of her life, Pitseolak Ashoona's subjects seemed frozen in place, as though they had been pared down and refined by long years of research and experimentation. Examples of this are *Crying Child* (1979, page 66) and *One Captive Bird* (1983, page 68). A few remarkable works, published

Before I start drawing,
I think what I am going to put down.
I just draw—sometimes from the past,
the things that I know.
I just draw.
Pitseolak Ashoona
interview with Marion Jackson, 1979

■

I never make my drawings balance on both sides
even though I try to.
After I finish them, I see that they are
only a little bit balanced.
Lucy Qinnuayuak
1978 Cape Dorset Print Catalogue, p. 59

■

Drawing out of your imagination
is a lot better to me anyway.
What you see in your head,
is what you try to put on drawing...
I try to make my drawings look attractive enough.
Kenojuak Ashevak
interview with Odette Leroux, 1991

posthumously, are veritable distillations of her work: *Migration towards Our Summer Camp* (1983, cat. 1984, page 68) presents the type of character found in her other prints, with shapes superimposed to suggest depth. Another late work, *To Rescue a Drowning Hunter* (1983, cat. 1984, page 67), takes up a theme that was dear to Pitseolak—the river. In this drawing, the artist has given a modern feel to her subject with effects of texture and the use of blue, a cold colour that emphasizes the dramatic nature of the composition.

Lucy Qinnuayuak

Lucy Qinnuayuak works in drawings and prints, and she has also explored acrylic painting. She creates striking scenes of the customs and environment of her people. Her brilliantly coloured art is expressive of a sensitive, often humorous realism. She has won international acclaim for her works on birds, which are her favourite subject. Her work can be simple and direct, or dense and complex; those shown here illustrate the great diversity of her talent. Intimist, expressive and revealing, Lucy Qinnuayuak's art shows audacity and innovation that is well served by her versatility and the diversity of her means of expression. In the work of this artist, the line reigns triumphant: organizing the space and delineating the subject, it creates both distance and emotion.

Lucy's early works show mainly birds and aspects of the traditional way of life. Towards the end of her artistic career, two works stand out clearly from the rest. *Fantasy Birds* (1977, page 88) is an acrylic work filled with lyricism and fantasy, in which birds and fabulous beings take on the colours of a dream. *Recollections* (1983, page 91) is a result of her experiments with the textures created by ink washes on stone or lithographic plates. These works are exceptional compositions which illustrate a rich and original dimension of Cape Dorset graphic art.

Figure 1
Kenojuak Ashevak,
1927-
THE ENCHANTED OWL
1960

stonecut, proof/50
printed by *Eegyvudluk
Pootoogook*, 1931-
stonecut by *Iyola
Kingwatsiak*, 1933-
on laid, rag paper
61 x 66 cm
Canadian Museum of
Civilization
Cape Dorset 1960,
no. 24

Kenojuak Ashevak

In the work of Kenojuak Ashevak, sculpture and drawing serve an extremely powerful vision that is fed by a vivid imagination. It guides her artistic concerns and acts as a catalyst for her inspiration. Her sense of form, assurance with colour, and taste for innovation are constantly leading her into new avenues: *No, I was never told to draw differently. No one ever told me to draw differently. I am changing my styles on my own perhaps because I know now how to draw. That's the way I am.* (interview with Odette Leroux, 1991)

Kenojuak Ashevak is famous around the world, thanks to her masterpiece *The Enchanted Owl* (1960, fig. 1). Her first work, *Rabbit Eating Seaweed* (1958, cat. 1959, fig. 2) foreshadows her concern with representing nature, which is a constant in her work. Throughout her entire career, she has borrowed motifs from nature—seaweed, leaves, flowers—and has juxtaposed these natural forms to create a play of contrasts. Some of her first prints, such as *A Complex of Birds* (1960, fig. 3), are notable for their treatment of fluid, airy forms as well as for their juxtaposition and interaction in space.

Jean Blodgett suggests in her book *Grasp Tight the Old Ways: Selections from the Klamer Family Collection of Inuit Art* that Kenojuak's artistic process emphasizes design over narrative content. Her art is first and foremost an appreciation of the beauty of the universe. She creates without a preconceived idea, developing her drawings by progressive strokes, until she is satisfied with the composition: *When I start drawing, I go along—and then I say to myself, I think it would look nice if I add something to it—if I put something here. That would make it look nice. That's how I do it. When I draw, I think a lot as I go along.* (interview with Marion Jackson, 1979)

Kenojuak's style has undergone a long progression, and *Birds and Foliage* (1970, fig. 4) is an important milestone, where abstraction reaches its peak and where, for the first

Figure 2
Kenojuak Ashevak,
1927-
RABBIT EATING
SEAWEED
1958

stencil, proof Gov't/30
printed by *Iyola
Kingwatsiak*, 1933-
on wove, kozo paper
22.5 x 60.7 cm
Canadian Museum of
Civilization
Cape Dorset 1959,
no. SS8

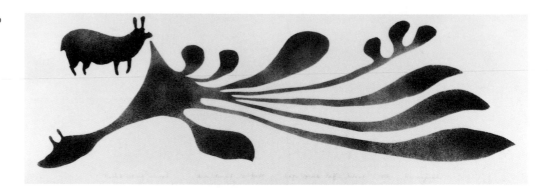

Figure 3
Kenojuak Ashevak,
1927-
COMPLEX OF BIRDS
1960

stonecut, proof Gov't
'B' (edition: 50)
printed by *Eegyvudluk
Pootoogook*, 1931-
on laid, rag paper
58.5 x 66 cm
Canadian Museum of
Civilization
Cape Dorset 1960,
no. 17

Figure 4
Kenojuak Ashevak,
1927-
BIRDS AND FOLLIAGE
1970

stonecut, proof III/50
printed by *Lukta
Qiatsuk*, 1928-
on laid, kozo paper
62 x 86.4 cm
Canadian Museum of
Civilization
Cape Dorset 1970,
no. 2

time, highly stylized leaves are incorporated into the work. In *Summer Owl* (1979, page 100), the realist-abstract composition presents an amalgamation of powerful motifs that fill up almost the entire space. Her talent as a colourist finds a fertile ground here. *The World Around Me* (1980, page 101) accentuates Kenojuak's pictorial message through a synthesis of recurring subjects. In sharp contrast, *Goddess of the Sky* (1980, page 97) and *Owl and Friends* (1980, page 103) mark a return to a more intimist, almost muted vision of the world. Starting from the face of the *Goddess of the Sky* and her traditional headdress, Kenojuak develops a purely imaginary design, without the slightest concern for realism. For Kenojuak, *Summer Owl* and *Owl and Friends* are closely related; the artist adds that she also sees a landscape, hills and sky in the works.

Kenojuak Ashevak seeks constantly to expand the boundaries of her art, without sacrificing her authenticity. Her determination, combined with her immense talent, her spontaneity and her aesthetic sense have contributed enormously to the wealth and diversity of Cape Dorset art.

Qaunak Mikkigak

Qaunak Mikkigak is a sculptor who has also experimented with jewellery making. Her artistic approach is based on her innate sense of form. Guided by her interest in art and crafts, she creates polyvalent, original sculptures drawn directly from her imagination or inspired by her emotions. The diversity of Qaunak Mikkigak's means of expression and her inimitable style reveal an accomplished artist who makes full use of her artistic resources. Her rich imagination, sustained by a keen aesthetic sense, contributes to expanding the range of Cape Dorset's artistic activities.

In sculpting, Qaunak Mikkigak has no preconceived ideas. Her subject emerges from the stone as she carves away at the block before her. Her vision alone inspires and guides her

hands: *I just carve out of my imagination.* (interview with Odette Leroux, 1991)

Initially, she sculpted simple subjects with spare forms, such as *Owl* (1965, page 117). Progressively, her compositions grew in volume and complexity. She introduced characters and animals or a combination of both, as shown in *Selfish Hunter* (1988, page 127), *Nanook Eating Sedna* (1988, page 129) and *The Real Woman* (1990, page 112). These compositions are beautifully balanced and the forms executed in a masterful way. *The Real Woman* shows a character frozen in time, draped in traditional ceremonial garb, invested with all her powers. This work shows the particular appeal that the representation of women has for Qaunak.

Sometimes she combines several subjects in totemic or superimposed forms. Certain compositions reveal a process in which realism is allied to abstraction, as in *Shaman* (circa 1977, page 122), *Tern Swooping Man and Woman* (circa 1987, page 125) and *Shaman Performing* (circa 1988, page 126). Qaunak admits to a particular interest in this style—*the pieces I value the most* (interview with Odette Leroux, 1991)—where her art is expressed with strength and eloquence. Representing the shaman in a totemic form amplifies his power and makes concrete the process of transformation. Two unusual compositions, *Reaching for Fish* (circa 1987, page 124) and *Sedna Frightened by Weird Creature* (1988, page 128), juxtapose subjects that are both similar and different, and reveal some favourite motifs of the artist. Apart from their fascinating appeal, these powerful works show an energy that is rare. The artist comments on the representation of the hand in the centre which gives pause for thought: *Yes, I made quite a few figures with hands. Because I like to make them as it is only hands that made us able to work.* (interview with Marion Jackson and Odette Leroux, 1992). Ovilu Tunnillie shares this point of view (page 237).

Sculpture, which Qaunak practices in solitude and

*It feels very good when you're comfortable
in feeling good about your carvings
especially when other people like your carvings.
There and then you know you can do a good carving
each and every time you begin one.*
Qaunak Mikkigak
interview with Odette Leroux, 1991

■

*In the beginning of my art,
I used to draw things that…I have heard about….
Today, I draw things that I know about personally.
I also try to improve in my drawings depicting things
that I know more about….
That is why my style has changed.*
Napachie Pootoogook
interview with Odette Leroux, 1991

silence, remains her preferred medium: *Yes, I find it easier to carve and I do enjoy it better.* (interview with Odette Leroux, 1991). But she doesn't deny her pleasure in creating jewellery: *I really enjoyed working at the jewellery shop [in Cape Dorset].* (interview with Marion Jackson, 1979) A jewellery-making competition entitled "The Things that Make Us Beautiful," organized and sponsored by the Department of Indian and Northern Affairs in 1976, first piqued her interest. The criteria of the competition required that the jewellery had to use only natural materials and Qaunak drew on her talents as seamstress, engraver and sculptor to create some vivid colourful entries. Since then, as a starting point for her jewellery, Qaunak carves faces that she decorates with utilitarian and decorative materials. Her pieces have a distinctive appearance, thanks to their unique combination of bold forms and the choice of materials.

Napachie Pootoogook

Napachie Pootoogook concentrates on drawings and prints, with some ventures into sculpture and acrylic painting. Much of her art has a narrative base, drawn from personal experience, historical events or social commentary. Her style has developed in five distinct phases: her early works (1960 to 1970); stories with a historical and social character (1978 to 1989); imaginary and fan-ciful scenes (1978 to 1990); intimist works on women in Inuit society (1989 and 1990); and studies in a realist-abstract style (1983 and 1990). The observations that Napachie Pootoogook makes through her pictorial work have contributed to an understanding of the economic and social history of the North, and diversified the means of expression available to the women of Cape Dorset.

A multitude of influences is clearly apparent during her initial period, in works like *Inuit Sea Dreams* (page 137) and *Bird Spirits* (page 139), both from 1960. Their colourful background corresponds to a style that was very popular in Cape

Dorset at the time. *Inuit Family Playing Ball* (1961, page 140), *Ball Game* (1966, cat. 1967, page 142), *Untitled* (1962, page 141) and *Birds Feeding* (1964, page 142) reveal the unmistakable influence of her mother, Pitseolak Ashoona, in their themes, motifs, compositional layout and choice of colours. This is most evident when Napachie's *Drawing of My Tent* (1982, page 149) is compared with Pitseolak's *The Critic* (circa 1963, fig. 5). *Whale Hunt* (circa 1970, page 144), a drawing in coloured pencil, reveals the artist's sensitivity in the use of line, stroke and colour. Her sense of composition translates skilfully the importance of the whale in traditional Inuit society.

On the other hand, Napachie's studies in a realist-abstract style differ radically from the rest of her work, and result from original aesthetic research. *Summer Scene* (1983, page 152) presents a realist-abstract landscape using a lithographic ink wash, a technique she experimented with under the direction of Don Phillips in 1983. *Majualajut (Up Through the Rough Shore Ice)* (1990, page 155) is innovative in its synthesis of subjects: the hatching strokes representing the ice floes create an animated and unusual space for the representation of this traditional motif.

Pitaloosie Saila

Pitaloosie Saila's art is realist, formal-abstract, direct and very powerful; her motifs command attention. Her paintings reveal her preoccupation with the reduction and stylization of forms. She has a distinctive approach in her stylistic development. Pitaloosie Saila excels in bringing the elements of her environment to life through her unique vision, sensitive perception and the concerns that guide her pictorial art.

Oopik Pitsiulak

Oopik Pitsiulak's sculpture is both intimist and innovative. Her respect for ancestral values, heightened aesthetic sense, creativity, enthusiasm and spontaneity have led to the emergence of new artistic trends in her work. Her unique way of organizing and integrating glass beads in her compositions lends a distinctiveness to her sculpture and brings a new dimension to Cape Dorset art. Her mode of expression affirms the wealth of cultural values and traditions, while paying tribute to her grandmother, the first source of her inspiration. With her lively creativity, Oopik has created original works of a very high artistic quality.

Figure 5
Pitseolak Ashoona,
1904-1983
THE CRITIC
circa 1963

graphite pencil on
wove paper
47.5 x 61 cm
signed
Gift of the Department
of Indian Affairs and
Northern
Development, 1989
National Gallery of
Canada, Ottawa,
Ontario

36404
(Photograph: National
Gallery of Canada)

You don't just do drawings...
you express yourself.
It is also a way of life, a part of life.
Life is sometimes heavy...
you have to be able to express yourself.
Some of it comes out through art....
I am just doing what I know how to do best.
Pitaloosie Saila
interview with Marion Jackson and Odette Leroux, 1992

■

My grandmother's ability to make things
is always coming back to me...
I have been thinking about her a lot more in the 1990s...
I made my artwork to show
what I have done before in my life.
Oopik Pitsiulak
interview with Marion Jackson and Odette Leroux, 1992

■

When I do something I take those out of my mind.
I use them [traditional stories] for my drawing,
but I do a lot more from my imagination.
Mayoreak Ashoona
interview with Odette Leroux, 1991

■

I get an image as to what I want to carve for a long while....
I try to see it in my mind's eye as to how it would look....
Sometimes an idea pops in my mind regarding
how it would look and [I] discard it if it doesn't seem good.
I try to have a complete picture in my mind first
before I finally start to carve a piece.
Ovilu Tunnillie
interview with Odette Leroux, 1991

Mayoreak Ashoona

For Mayoreak Ashoona, sculpture represents an occasional diversion from the drawings and prints that are her mainstay. Her work reflects her thoughts and life experiences. A historian at heart, Mayoreak is aware of the importance of documentation, to the point that she makes it her duty to keep a record of all the traditions so they can be passed down intact from one generation to the next: *I started writing while thinking of the future, for my children and the museum. It's about myself since I do not wish to keep on just living only the Inuit way.... It tells all about my work. I added everything that I do on a daily basis.* (interview with Marion Jackson and Odette Leroux, 1992)

Her favourite subjects are drawn from her daily life and the way of life she seeks to preserve. *When I do a drawing, I draw from my head—what I'm thinking.... It has to come from a person's mind. That's why it's hard—especially if you want to make it look real.* (interview with Marion Jackson, 1979)

Mayoreak's work communicates her appreciation of the beauty of the Arctic land and the culture and customs of her people. Her mode of expression is supported by documentation that helps understand her work and her aesthetic process.

Mayoreak's early works from the end of the 1970s are highly animated and remarkably fresh, notably because of the choice of pastel tones that is so surprising at first view. *Shore Birds* (1978, page 200) is an original composition, without a precise structure but with a high degree of fantasy. It seems to have been born of her need for experimentation and her interest in colour. In the same vein, *Tornaq* (1977, cat. 1978, page 203) comes from a dream of animals represented through a glass. These two works blend fluid realist and abstract forms to create movement. In contrast, *Bear Spirit* (1979, page 205) evokes solidity, even though its source is the imagination, because it is organized in realist motifs crossed with surrealism.

Figure 6
Oopik Pitsiulak, 1946-
WOMAN CHILD
1980

dark green stone
28.5 x 42.6 x 30 cm
signed
Collection: West Baffin
Eskimo Co-operative
Ltd., on loan to the
McMichael Canadian
Art Collection,
Kleinburg, Ontario
GR4300
(Photograph: Larry
Ostrom, Westport,
Ontario)

Ovilu Tunnillie

Highly personalized, the sculpture of Ovilu Tunnillie closely espouses her experience and philosophy of life. Her creativity and determination, her need for self-affirmation, her pride in her origins and her strong personality imbue and sustain her artistic expression. Among her thematic subjects, several translate her personal life and vision of the world, some attest to traditional or contemporary values, while others deliver a social message. Ovilu's vivid imagination and innovative sense have made a major contribution to the creation of an original body of work that has ventured outside the usual channels. She experiments freely, producing strong works that are filled with freshness and audacity. She has also produced some jewellery.

THE WORK OF THESE WOMEN draws on several common themes.

As for any artist, personal experience is a primary source of inspiration. Pitaloosie Saila captures memories on canvas in *My Dolls* (1967, cat. 1968, page 163) and *Family of Twins* (1971, page 168). The daring, modern composition of *My Dolls* is based on a formal balance, achieved by an economy of means, where the left-hand line delineates the scene and pinpoints the subject. *Family of Twins* is also inspired by recollections of her own childhood. The energy of the drawing and the stylization of the forms and lines are ideally suited to the subject.

The glass beadwork of Oopik Pitsiulak's grandmother has been a great inspiration in her creative process. She recalls a precious memory of her grandmother: *I [often] think of my grandmother and the beadwork she used to do. As I was doing the carving, I thought to myself: 'Now I wonder if it would look really nice if I put beadwork on it?' I thought of it that way with the woman I was carving while thinking of my grandmother's work. I kept wondering how it would look if I put beadwork on it so I went ahead and put beadwork on it.*

(interview with Marion Jackson and Odette Leroux, 1992)

In 1990, Oopik's first small sculptures with glass beads were designed to be self-portraits. As with other Cape Dorset artists, her imagination feeds her subjects: *I tend to push myself when I carve certain shapes by telling myself that you have to show it. First of all, I'll think about how it's going to look if I carve it this way or that way. Then I have to go through with it in order to finish it well, just as I'd imagined it to be in the beginning. This is my style of carving.* (interview with Marion Jackson and Odette Leroux, 1992)

Two styles overlap in Oopik's art: one merely suggests the form and the detail through an almost abstract approach, while the other captures the subject painstakingly in its slightest detail. *Oopik Thinking* (1990, page 194) and *Oopik Softening the Skin* (1990, page 193) are roughly modelled, suggesting rather than defining the forms, but they are powerful despite their small size. The glass beadwork that decorates the stone adds a note of gaiety and the curve of the dress lends an indisputably feminine appearance to the pieces and a nobility to the subject. By contrast, *Oopik Going for Water* (1990, page 188) is carved in minute detail. The sculpture is impressive in its form and expressive in its detail. The very animated face and hair reinforce the elegance and dynamism of the work. Several elements have a particular appeal: the glass beads integrated into the hair of mother and child as well as into the *amauti* and sealskin pail; the *amauti* itself and its maternal hood; and the decorative motifs. The ingenious integration of the children and the rendering of their forms completes this masterpiece. *Woman Child* (1980, fig. 6) allows us to appreciate the earlier work of the artist while it confirms her virtuosity of form.

In *My Mother and Myself* (1990, page 238) and *This Has Touched My Life* (1991-1992, page 239), Ovilu Tunnillie traces parallels between her life in the Arctic and her childhood in the South. Each of these works is accompanied by an account of the event; both illustrate personal experiences that have marked her. Although both are set in the context of the 1950s, the time during which these events took place, the first is traditional and static in its style, while the second is more modern because of the dynamic representation of the women and the suppleness of their clothing.

A larger source of inspiration for their work is the world of the Inuit woman. Through their art the artists paint a composite portrait of the Inuit woman and offer a glimpse of the battle this woman has waged within her society to preserve traditional values while the modern world unfolds before her. Each of these artists uncovers a different facet of the Inuit woman. Pitseolak's portrayals of women are revealing and imaginative. *Tattooed Woman* (1963, page 51) and *The Shaman's Wife* (1980, page 66) are striking examples of her expressionism, their intensity heightened by the choice of voluminous shapes and the evocative power of the tattoos. *Tattooed Woman* in particular demonstrates an innate sense of abstraction and an economy of means, as do *Crossing the River* (1967, page 52) and *Old Women Speak of Owl* (1974, page 62). These compositions show the artist's delicacy of execution and her incomparable sense of symmetry and balance.

In Lucy Qinnuayuak's work, women occupy a privileged place, appearing in diverse roles such as *Women Carrying Fish* (1972, page 83) and *Women and Children* (circa 1973, page 82). *Pilatuktu (Skinning the Seal;* 1979, page 90) and *Bird Fantasy* (1977-1978, page 70) show the power of the woman in traditional Inuit society, while also illustrating her tasks. Lucy was introduced to acrylic painting by artist K. M. Graham, who painted in Cape Dorset during 1976 and 1977, and she used the medium to good effect in *Two Women Playing* (1977, page 81). This work is an ode to play set against a yellow/orange-hued background that emphasizes all of the forms, especially the half-moon shapes that echo the curves of the ball in the game.

In another acrylic painting, *Women and Owls* (1977, page 84), birds perched on fluid and vaporous forms that symbolize plants dominate the scene while two women dressed in their *amautiit* figure humbly in the central panel.

The woman's face is a recurring central motif in Kenojuak Ashevak's pictorial work from 1974 on. In *The World Around Me* (1980, page 101), the female face is surrounded by leaves, owls, birds and fish, a synthesis of the people, the land and the animals of the Arctic. *The Goddess of the Sky* (1980, page 97) expresses the same stylistic idea. Qaunak Mikkigak's favourite theme is the human being and in particular the woman. Her first sculpture was a head for a doll, a subject that had a major significance for her. *Tern Swooping Man and Woman* (circa 1987, page 125) and *The Real Woman* (1990, page 112) are expressive, well-balanced and refined works.

The themes of the woman and the mother with children predominate in Pitaloosie's work: *I tend to draw images of women because there used to be a group of women all the time, back then, while the men were always gone. Perhaps that's why I draw them a lot, while they're busy in their work. Women used to get together a lot. At least, in my house. Especially around the elder women whose daughters-in-law tended to be around her. She'd be teaching them things such as sewing clothes. I do remember a lot of those times.* (interview with Odette Leroux, 1991) Pitaloosie's female subjects are very revealing. *Young Girl and Birds* (1970, page 166) presents a well-marked face whose forms are clear and precise. The figure in *Woman* (1970, page 167) is both abstract and realistic and filled with rare energy. The articulation of forms and positioning of the subject in this work made it stand out from other works by Cape Dorset women, particularly at the time of its creation.

The mother and child subject serves as a pretext for representing the various styles of traditional dress or for expressing the affection, tenderness and security given to the child,

explicit in *Arctic Madonna* (1980, page 170), *Affectionate Mother* (1985, page 174) and *Young Mother and Children* (1985, page 179). In *Woman Proudly Sewing* (1988, page 187), the principal character has an imposing, almost monumental form. In contrast, in *Changing Traditions* (1991, page 185), our attention is drawn to the three styles of clothing worn by three generations. The lengthened forms in this composition, bordering on expressionism, contrast with the imposing forms created by the curves of *Woman Proudly Sewing*. The innovative forms of *Changing Traditions* are perhaps the announcement of a new stylistic trend in Pitaloosie's work.

Mayoreak's graphic art favours the subject of the Inuit woman going about her daily work: *[I portray] the woman's work today, mainly when the men come home from hunting…. Then I would imagine the things that women do today.* (interview with Odette Leroux, 1991) *Putting Up the Tent* (1981, page 206), *Cleaning Fish* (1981, page 206) and *Putting Up the Tent* (1982, page 196) show the same sober stylistic trend. In these works, the details are drawn in pencil, while pastel shades enhance their intensity. These highly accomplished works hold a significant place in her production. *The New Kamiks* (1982, page 208) is a realist drawing, unlike *Preparing Skins for Kayak* (1982, page 208), which is stylized, yet the works complement each other. *Sharpening the Ulu* (1989, page 218) is a work of great simplicity and sobriety. In the use of stonecut, all of these works illustrate another of the artist's processes, much more static and cold. It is tempting to assume that some of the above works might be autobiographical.

Napachie Pootoogook also portrays women in Inuit society. Whether in *Woman Today* (1989, page 157), *My New Accordion* (1989, page 151) or *My Daughter's First Steps* (1990, page 154), her works have common characteristics: the bearing of the women, a face in profile, braided hair, the wearing of traditional clothing—the *amauti* with its hood as well as *kamiik*—the unusual positioning of the legs and the importance given to hands. Always in close-up, the woman fills up almost the entire space and the brilliance of the contrasting colours draws the eye. A strong feeling of tenderness and maternal solicitude emanates from these works. The remarkable landscape adds a dramatic note in counterpoint to the central figure of the mother in *My Daughter's First Steps*. It is relevant to add that *My New Accordion* is a self-portrait, according to Jean Blodgett in *In Cape Dorset We Do It This Way: Three Decades of Inuit Printmaking*.

TRADITIONAL WAYS OF LIFE, rites and beliefs are also central themes in Inuit art. Like any contemporary artist, the women use their art to register their past, display their preoccupations and record their experiences of present-day life in their society. *Summer Tent of Old* (1969, page 58), *Our Camp* (1974, page 61) and *Family Camping in Tuniit Ruins* (1976, page 65) all bear Pitseolak Ashoona's trademarks: similarly shaped rocks that structure the composition, and the use of shades of black, brown and ochre. Sometimes, everyday objects appear arbitrarily in her pictures, as is the case in *Bird with Avataq (Float)*(1970, cat. 1971, page 59). At other moments, the composition accentuates the presence and power of the main subject, as in *Bear Attacking Seal* (1973, page 60).

Play, animation and mirth are omnipresent in Pitseolak's engravings, especially *Women Juggling Stones* (1967, cat. 1968, page 57) and *Woman with Goslings* (1974, page 63). These works also show the artist's fondness for dark tones in her stonecuts and prints.

Lucy Qinnuayuak's personal world is apparent in her work. *Camp Scene* (circa 1972, page 80) is a very delicately drawn work that uses lines and forms to create an illusion of depth. *Umiak, Kayak and Birds* (circa 1972, page 78) effectively recalls the vastness of the Arctic seascape. The position of the sailboat, the strokes of the sail and the curves of the waves lend a tremendous

vitality to the composition. *Dancers and Gramophone* (circa 1972, page 79) offers a definite sense of joy and gaiety. Cool tones are dominant. These drawings illustrate the rich vocabulary of the artist.

Acrylic painting allowed Lucy to explore another dimension of her artistic talent. *Fish Weir* (1977, page 87) is a radical departure from her previous compositions, with its colourful style and multiple textures. Generally, her acrylic works feature a multitude of subjects in animated compositions; the space is organized by horizontal and vertical bands, while curves isolate the various components. For example, two high-perched birds seem to watch over several juxtaposed scenes in *Camp Scene with Animals and Birds* (1977, page 86). *Hunters, Bears and Seals* (1977, page 85) shows the same dynamism.

Napachie portrays the traditional way of life in works like *Spring Dance* (1979, page 146), *The River Route* (1989, page 153) and *Mending the Summer Tent* (1989, page 150). The use of varied textures, the drawing strokes and cold colours accentuate the dramatic aspect of the two latter compositions, while demonstrating the artist's sense of plasticity. These realist landscapes use traditional motifs in a modern way.

SOME OF THE ARTISTS use social or historical commentary to illuminate the traditional. For instance, Napachie drew on her knowledge of historical events to create *Atachiealuk's Battle* (1978, page 143) and *Nascopie Reef* (1989, page 132). This interest in an historical perspective makes Napachie distinct among Cape Dorset artists. *The First Policeman I Saw* (1978, page 145) and *Whaler's Exchange* (1989, page 156) record the arrival of white men and illustrate the impact of outside influences on the Inuit society. Napachie's sense of story, admirably served by her sure technique and a great power of evocation, comes through clearly in these striking works.

For others, like Ovilu Tunnillie, the impact of Southern culture is a compelling subject. *At one point in my life when I*

Figure 7
Ovilu Tunnillie, 1949-
THE FOOTBALL
PLAYERS
circa 1990

green stone and ivory
61 x 38 x 22.8 cm
unsigned
Collection: Dr. and
Mrs. Albert Yuzpe,
London, Ontario
(Photograph: Jackie
Nobel, London,
Ontario)

was growing up, I remember becoming aware and that my ways or what I knew were more about white people.... Right now the white ways I knew as I became aware of things is more distinct in my memory than the traditional memories I have in my mind.... I was born Inuit traditionally, but the Inuit traditional style is like in a back burner for me. (interview with Odette Leroux, 1991) Because of her experience living in the South, Ovilu takes a new look at southern society. This is especially apparent in the introduction of nudes. Ovilu created *Woman on High Heels* (1987, page 234) from memory. The sense of forms and proportions and the placement of legs and hands make this a distinctive work. She has also represented athletes in *Football Player* (1981, page 230), *The Football Players* (circa 1990, fig. 7) and *Skater* (1988, page 236). The posture of the figures in these works emphasizes movement and sometimes reveals a humorous intent.

Ovilu also manifests her concern with the ravages of alcoholism in the communities of the North, and she delivers a very relevant, unbiased commentary on this situation. In *Thought Creates Meaning* (circa 1980, page 229), a hand symbolizes the grasp of alcohol on her people. As in *Woman Passed Out* (1987, page 235), this work forcefully transmits her message.

THE WORLD OF THE ARTISTS also embraces the mythology that underlies traditional Inuit society. Ovilu Tunnillie uses her art to represent myths, tales and customs from her culture, such as the stories about the shaman and the sea goddess. However, it is interesting to note that she is reserved of delving more deeply into these subjects, or of going beyond the anecdotal stage. She is not alone: this particular trait is common to these women artists of Cape Dorset, who nonetheless like to represent the mythical creatures. *Shaman Appears* (page 220), which dates from the 1970s, is an extraordinary piece whose form, pose, detail and modelling of the elements excels in rendering the power of the subject. In *Seaman, Seawoman and Fish* (circa 1981, page 231), the complexity of the composition, its formal balance, the preciseness of anatomical detail and the treatment of textures demonstrate an accomplished mastery of form. *Taleelayu* (1982-1983, page 232) is a marvel of voluptuousness thanks to its powerful volumes and the sensual charm of the sculpted curves. Mythology seems to be much less important in Cape Dorset than in other communities such as Baker Lake, however.

Pitaloosie has occasionally drawn her perception of the sea goddess or other uncommon subjects in a purely imaginary fashion. *Sedna with Fish* (1985, page 175) and *Out of the Sea* (1986, page 180), two compositions in close-up, are filled with sensuality, while *Flight of Fantasy* (1988, page 183) shows great restraint. Animated by the same movement, these works are distinctive in their individual character.

Pitseolak Ashoona with *The Shaman's Wife* (1980, page 66) and Qaunak Mikkigak with *Shaman* (circa 1977, page 122) and *Shaman Performing* (circa 1988, page 126) also explored the same theme.

THE ARCTIC LANDSCAPE is perhaps the most vivid common denominator in the work of these Cape Dorset women. The Far North is a fascinating country: its land, space, light and colour have a striking beauty which has inspired several contemporary Canadian artists. It is not surprising that such powerful surroundings have nourished Inuit artists too. Contemporary Inuit art has a close bond with nature; all of its subjects relate to the land and its people.

Mayoreak uses the vast landscape to good effect in her attempts to describe the multiple facets of the ancestral lifestyle, as shown in two works that are related by drawing style, pastel colours, choice of subject and representation of the land: *First Goose Hunt* (1979, page 205) and *Caribou in the Distance* (1980, page 209).

Kenojuak's art reveals her interest in nature and the land. The sculpture *Mother Nature* (1980-1982, page 104) shows a concern for detail that was latent in her previous works. *Bird Landscape* (1982, page 105) is a transitional work that unites all the elements of a realist-abstract landscape using precise draughtsmanship and pastel tones. *Timiatjuak (Large Birds;* 1987, page 92) illustrates a first attempt to seize concrete reality. Two birds in movement occupy the foreground, while the background shows a majestic landscape of land, water, mountains and sky. *Proud Wolf Pack* (1990, page 108) is a logical continuation of this attempt.

Nunavut Qajanartuk (Our Beautiful Land) (1990, page 109) reflects a new cycle in the artist's aesthetic research. While reiterating Kenojuak's love of the Northern landscape, this work also expresses her concern for the occupants of the Arctic territory and for their ancestral culture. She continues to explore this theme in *Nunavut* (1992, page 110), a masterpiece in which the artist embraces the entire Arctic land by illustrating the passing seasons and the cycle of night and day, within a circle bordered by hills and vast empty spaces that hint at the third dimension.

The birds that inhabit this sweeping land are one of the favourite subjects of these women. Some of their creatures, of course, are pure inventions and have fantastic shapes and colours.

In her drawings, Pitseolak Ashoona gives free rein to her talents as a colourist. As is evident in *Gay Bird* (1967, page 53), *First Bird of Spring* (1975, page 64) and *Many-Winged Bird* (1983, page 69), her colour palette has lightened progressively over the years and her birds have become all the more original and expressive as a result. As with her human portraits, she depicts the birds in front and side views, with the exception of *Many-Winged Bird* who unfolds his wings from the back.

Lucy Qinnuayuak represented, realistically or fancifully,

bird forms in a variety of poses. *Family of Birds* (1963, page 74) is an unusual and detailed work: the bulging eyes of the bird add to its comical expression and the skilful placement of forms lends a great deal of movement to the composition. In contrast, the interest of *Two Birds* (1968, page 75) lies in its stationary and stylized elegance of forms. *Spectator Birds* (1969, cat. 1970, page 76) and *Composition* (1972, page 80) are distinctive in their airy, dynamic and imaginative composition that attests to Lucy's creativity. She achieves an optical illusion in *Tulukara* (*Young Raven*) (1977, page 89) and *A Display of Feathers* (1982, page 90): the birds' feet, well defined and solidly anchored on the ground, contrast with the impression of movement created by the network of lines that make up their bodies.

Kenojuak likes to draw birds, and the owl, her subject of choice, is shown in every possible aspect throughout her work. *Owl* (date unknown, page 99), a refined sculpture with simple lines, is majestic in its volume and the movement that animates it. *Birds* (1969, page 102) constitutes a synthesis of the owl as it has been developed throughout the artist's work, and is a superb example of Kenojuak's mastery of three-dimensional forms. The attention to detail is impressive, and the eyes are particularly effective: even in stone the artist has managed to convey their piercing quality.

Qaunak Mikkigak's approach to drawing differs considerably from the approach she uses in her sculpture and jewellery making, and her graphic works are most often studies of birds. She works principally from reflection and observation. As drawing forms the basis of her compositions, line and stroke play several roles, serving to circumscribe fluid and moving forms, to suggest volumes and to give texture to elements. Despite their linear nature, the works *Spring Geese* (1980, page 121), *First Goose of the Spring* (1981, page 123) and *Geese in Spring* (1981, page 123) are filled with remarkable freshness, simplicity and beauty.

The bird is Pitaloosie Saila's favourite motif and it runs through her work, both as central element and as an incidental part of the compositions. From 1984 on, she is very adventurous in her treatments. Pitaloosie gives her winged subjects a distinct personality and fills up most of the space with them, striving to portray their magnetism and seductive power. *Bird in Morning Mist* (1984, page 170) shows a discreet, studied modernism. The predominance of the subject, the spareness and organization of forms that are both realistic and abstract, the rendering of textures and skilful use of colour all give a remarkable beauty to this work. *Moulting Owl* (1985, page 181) is executed in flat tones, but the delineation of the subject in blue and the rendering of the plumage creates an effect of volume. *Red-Necked Loon* (1988, page 184) defines in a more structured manner the principal parts of the body. *Sea Bird* (1984, page 171) and *Nestling* (1985, page 176) are at once similar and distinct in their rendering of tones and textures and the dynamism of forms.

Birds return often in Mayoreak Ashoona's iconography. *Nocturnal Falcon* (1989, page 217) is a majestic and aesthetically valuable work. The bird fills most of the space; it is seen from the back, wings spread, head up, its body filled with textures and folds in which the light plays. The black background adds to the dramatic character of the composition, detaching the silhouette of the bird. *Two Arctic Murres* (1987, page 218) is a study of the subject; they are seen again, this time in action, in *Flight Over Fish Lake* (1987, page 215).

Mayoreak sculpts on occasion. *Seagull Eating Char at the River* (1989, page 216), vigorously sculpted, is an impressive work that is faithful to her aesthetic preoccupations. *Inniutik (Drying Rack)* (1990-1991, page 219), an authentic traditional drying rack, makes us tangibly aware of the customs of her family: *It is my sculpture of the skin thawing out on the rack just like my parents used to do. That sculpture is in reality the way my parents used to live.* (interview with Marion Jackson and Odette Leroux, 1992)

Birds also number among Ovilu Tunnillie's preferred themes. *Composition of Owls* (circa 1977, page 228) is a major work, characteristic of her first compositions, in a heavy, dense sculptural mass. *Owl* (circa 1979, page 228), in high relief, reveals a certain lightening of form, which can be attributed to the lines of the face and the movement of the feet. *Hawk Taking Off* (circa 1987, page 233) is remarkable in the rendering of the wings—one of Ovilu's particular talents—which are very skilfully executed. The fluid, airy forms, dynamism and movement, compositional audacity and sculptural vigour endow *Hawk Eating Arctic Char* (1987-1989, fig. 8) with elegance and beauty. In *Hawk Landed* (circa 1989, page 237), the rendering of feet and beak animate and personify the subject.

Animals, on the other hand, do not seem to appeal to the women. Although the Inuit depend on animals for their survival and although animals are a major subject for male artists, very few animals are included in the women's work. Ovilu Tunnillie is an exception. She made a small piece, *Man and Bear* (1974-1976, page 226), during a jewellery-making workshop, and has a particular affection for dogs, which she has observed carefully. *Dogs Fighting* (circa 1975, page 227) was done in high relief, unlike most of the sculptures, which are generally in the round.

Aʟᴛʜᴏᴜɢʜ ᴛʜᴇ ᴄᴀᴘᴇ ᴅᴏʀsᴇᴛ ᴡᴏᴍᴇɴ artists focus so intensely on the world they live in, they also create unusual and unique pieces that offer an entree into the world of the imagination. Each of them has her own way of expressing her most intimate world. Kenojuak's highly original works, *Spirit Helpers* (1989, page 106) and *Spirits at Night* (1989, page 107), are dreamlike, even if the artist herself denies it: *If I drew what I dream, some of them would be perhaps too remarkable.* (interview with Odette Leroux, 1991). The two multiform compositions are certainly unusual, although the predominant elements of Kenojuak's art are still discernible.

Figure 8
Ovilu Tunnillie, 1949-
Hᴀᴡᴋ Eᴀᴛɪɴɢ
Aʀᴄᴛɪᴄ Cʜᴀʀ
1987–1989

grey-green stone
36.8 x 48.2 x 26.1 cm
unsigned
Collection: General
Electric Canada Inc.,
Mississauga, Ontario
(Photograph: Thomas
Moore, Toronto,
Ontario)

Head with Hands and Webbed Feet (1991, page 130) and *Head with Hands* (1991, page 131) represent a similar current in Qaunak's work, while *Bear Spirit* (1979, page 205) is an example of Mayoreak's use of the imagination.

Purely fictitious works by Napachie Pootoogook are rare: *Carried Off by a Bird* (1980, page 147) and *Flying Near the Rainbow* (1980, page 148) are examples. One of their characteristics is their unusual composition. The action and movement are made unreal to capture the viewer's attention and the artist uses a warm orange shade, probably to emphasize the element of surprise.

Pitaloosie Saila's studies of imaginary subjects, expressed in a fantasy-like, even surreal fashion, are quite surprising. *Some of [my drawings] are from my own imagination and some are from stories that I've heard. Some of what I've seen that I remember.* (interview with Odette Leroux, 1991) *Courting Owl* (1985, page 172) is an astonishing bird. In *Wolf Spirit* (1987, page 182) the juxtaposed, superimposed and entangled body forms are both abstract and stylized, and *Sheltered Owl* (1987, page 183) is equally striking.

THESE ARTISTS have worked in isolation, unaware of major artistic trends and developments around the world. In light of this fact, Pitaloosie Saila's achievement is quite exceptional. Her work seems to show the stylistic influence of African art and of Picasso. In *Inuit Leader* (1972, page 169), for example, the singular representation of the face has been ascribed to the influence of Picasso, but the artist says: *I saw some of his drawings, and they are not like mine. He used to do a lot of naked people. I never did any naked people.* (interview with Marion Jackson, 1979). Nonetheless, Pitaloosie has followed a process similar to that of Picasso during the 1930s, when he deconstructed and transposed his motifs. Pitaloosie simply drew the face of *Inuit Leader* and bordered it with its inverted

shadow: *I drew it as a shadow, part of the face in the dark. As if the homes in those days were not well-lighted.* (interview with Marion Jackson and Odette Leroux, 1992). The face is treated in flat tones, with a uniform application of colour, which brings it out in two dimensions and creates a very interesting ambiguity. The curved line circumscribes and amplifies the volumes, while the treatment of textures and the layers of colour animate the subject. Worth noting are the facial tattoos, which are a very important Inuit custom

Woman and Snow Bird (1973, page 158) and *Woman of Old* (1984, page 174) are inspired by the same desire to deconstruct the face, presenting it simultaneously in profile and front view. The two compositions are quite different: the first uses a realistic approach, with repeated motifs of the hair and the bird, while the second is abstract. Here the purification of form has reached its peak: the play of textures gives relief and presence to this almost unreal character, rare in Inuit art.

THE CREATIVE VISION and vibrant imagination of these artists has helped them translate their emotions and concerns, as women and as members of the Inuit community, in the face of their deteriorating environment and disappearing customs and culture. The diversity of the themes, the styles adopted and the media exploited all attest to the vitality of their artistic expression. Although inspired by traditional aesthetic values, these women have been able to innovate and to constantly recreate colours and forms. Their enormous talent, coupled with boundless enthusiasm and determination, has led to the enrichment of a unique dimension of contemporary Canadian art.

The Voices of Inuit Women

Marion E. Jackson

THE LAST HALF OF THE TWENTIETH CENTURY has been marked by sweeping changes globally and within the Inuit culture as well. Nowhere is this change more evident than in the emerging roles of Inuit women. The appearance of Third World nations as new players on the world stage and the emergence of an internationally based feminist movement have coincided with a period of profound cultural change in Canada's North. For Inuit women, this period has been one not only of moving from the land to the settlements, from the traditional living patterns to the modern, but also of embracing new roles and new responsibilities within their culture and on the intersections where their culture interfaces with those of southern Canada and the wider world.

During the past forty years, the visual arts have given the Inuit woman new opportunities for economic independence—freeing her from her traditional role as supporter of the hunter—and have also given her new avenues for expression. In the expanding literature on Inuit art and culture and in discussions of the profound changes reshaping Canada's North, however, rarely are the voices of interpretation those of native Inuit, and even more rarely are they the voices of Inuit women. The writings that follow, therefore, are extraordinary, unique in the fresh insight they offer into the experience of modern Inuit women.

The seven Cape Dorset women artists and three Inuit women leaders whose writing appears in this book convey directly and unpretentiously the values, aspirations and quiet wisdom of women whose roots lie deeply within the traditional Inuit culture. All of these women were born within the last sixty-five years and all have experienced the imposition on their culture of the powerful imperatives of the expanding industrialized world. Their words allow readers new insight into the concerns, hopes, goals and everyday demands that give structure and meaning to the lives of these women artists and that provide the context and motivation for the art of Cape Dorset women. The reader is offered access to a life experience from the perspective of those most intimately engaged in that experience.

New directions within both the Inuit culture and the museum community have combined to make this writing possible. In the traditional Inuit culture where the norms of expression were oral, not literary, and where reflective self-expression (particularly among women) was subordinated to the intentions of the community, there were few opportunities or incentives for Inuit women to document in writing their personal concerns and ideas. Traditionally, Inuit women were trained to be patient and self-contained, competent, and unassertive except within their own domain inside the tent or igloo or modern "prefab" home. Neither asserting oneself publicly nor offering one's written reflections for publication were familiar or comfortable activities for Inuit women raised in the traditional culture. It is only recently that a few Inuit leaders such as Minnie Aodla Freeman and Mary Cmkovich have been publishing their own ideas and experiences and encouraging other Inuit women to do the same.

At the same time, expectations and practices within the museum community are undergoing change as well. Museums have a long history of interpreting aboriginal art from the "objective" perspective of trained museum professionals and presenting it from a clearly defined curatorial perspective. Only recently have museums begun to engage artists and other aboriginal thinkers in the interpretation of aboriginal arts. The Canadian Museum of Civilization's 1992 exhibition *Indigena* was one of the first major museum exhibitions to be developed totally from an aboriginal perspective.

The voices of these Inuit women, therefore, emerge in the context of these complementary changes within the Inuit culture and within the museum community. Modern Inuit women are no longer culturally bound to defer quietly and patiently while their interests are interpreted and represented by others, and no longer do principal museums turn exclusively to non-Inuit professionals for interpretation of the lives and art of Inuit artists. An alternative model is emerging which acknowledges that understanding is enriched by an awareness of the values and intentions of the artists. In this model, the curator (whether from within the culture or without) attempts not so much to impose a curatorial viewpoint as to facilitate communication between artists and audience and to acknowledge the complexity of the human experience embodied in the works of art.

The writing in this book reflects that complexity as well. Just as the works of art differ markedly from one artist to another, so too does the writing. Even though the traditional Inuit lifestyle has been the dominant experience of all of these women, each voice presents an individual view, an individual set of experiences and individual goals.

The work of the artists—both the writing and the art—is arranged in an order proceeding from the older artists to the younger. The two most senior artists in this exhibition—Lucy Qinnuayuak and Pitseolak Ashoona—are no longer living and have not written for this book. They are represented, however, by their energetic graphic works, by quotations from other sources, and by memories of them written by others. They are well remembered by the younger artists who carry forward the legacy which they and their peers began in Cape Dorset nearly half a century ago.

The book concludes with the writings of three Inuit leaders—Ann Meekitjuk Hanson, Annie Manning and Minnie Aodla Freeman. Ann Meekitjuk Hanson has travelled widely and visited extensively with elders throughout the Northwest Territories. Her poetic reflection is written not from the perspective of creating art but from the perspective of appreciating the role of art in preserving the Inuit culture. Annie Manning likewise sees the importance of the arts in fostering pride and identity among young people. She reflects on her own life experience in the changing North and describes her own sense of responsibility as a modern Inuk woman. Writer Minnie Aodla Freeman muses on the socialization of young women and the adaptation of women's roles within Inuit culture.

Familiarity with "outside" cultures varies considerably among the artists. Kenojuak Ashevak, the senior living artist in this group, has had opportunities to travel internationally in connection with her art, and she has received extensive recognition for her artistic achievement. Her autobiographical musings span the course of her life from birth to the present day and convey her clear sense of her identity within the traditional culture. Ovilu Tunnillie and Pitaloosie Saila, on the other hand, spent several formative childhood years in hospitals in southern Canada and even learned some English before returning to camp life on Baffin Island. Both of these artists offer impressions of their painful experiences.

By contrast, some artists in this group have had relatively little experience with the "outside" world. Napachie Pootoogook and Mayoreak Ashoona (daughter and daughter-in-law, respectively, of Pitseolak Ashoona) have travelled very little outside the North, and their work is strongly focused on their experience of the traditional culture. Mayoreak Ashoona lives today at the same outpost camp where she was born nearly fifty years ago.

None of the writers presumes to speak for others, even in her own community, or to assert privilege for her own view.

Each artist sees her life and her art from a unique perspective. The writing of Qaunak Mikkigak and Oopik Pitsiulak, for example, contains thoughtful reflections on the impact of their early experiences on the decisions they have made in their later lives. Qaunak Mikkigak writes of her early life experiences and reflects on the importance of early nurturing, while Oopik Pitsiulak considers the changing roles of Inuit women and pays tribute to the strength of women of earlier generations—such as her grandmother—whose composure, confidence and strength she admires.

It is in the combination of these perspectives that a reader gains access to the fullness of memories, the range of possibilities and the multiple aspirations held by Cape Dorset women. Their voices are dignified, direct, unpretentious and honest, and stand as a tribute to the women who wrote them and to the culture in which these women were nourished. That these voices were invited to accompany the art is a tribute as well to the Canadian Museum of Civilization in its commitment to enabling these women artists to speak for themselves.

It may be tempting to view the emergence of Inuit women in leadership roles and the emergence of independent women artists and writers not only as a new phenomenon but also as evidence of women's movement from positions of subordination to positions of more independence and power in the Inuit culture. That would be misleading. The role of women in Inuit culture has always been one of strength. They have always provided stability, nourished the youngest members and passed to them the accumulated wisdom of the culture. Though the present is clearly a time of transition, this role is still valid today. These artists and others of their generation are the last to fully experience life on the land. As artists, writers and emerging leaders, Inuit women still embrace women's traditional responsibilities—responsibilities for remembering the past, for bringing safety and grace to the present and for passing on values and wisdom for use in the future. That, ultimately, is the goal of both the art and the writings of these Cape Dorset artists. As evidenced in both, these women shoulder these important responsibilities with dignity and pride and with the humility one feels when one sees one's own role as integral to, yet integrated within, a greater whole.

Given the extraordinary nature of these writings, a postscript regarding the method used in editing is appropriate. It was my privilege to work with the manuscripts prepared by the artists and to review edited texts with each of them. While I did make minor editorial changes in the English translations, such changes were minimal and my intent at all times was to preserve both the substance and the spirit of the original expression.

Inuit Women Artists

Pitseolak Ashoona

When I first started doing the drawings I did all the work
in black and brown, and I still like these two colours,
although now we are using many coloured pens.
Jim said to draw the old ways in bright colours.

Quote by Pitseolak Ashoona
from Dorothy Harley Eber's
book, *Pitseolak: Pictures out of
My Life*.

Pitseolak Ashoona
1904–1983

Born on Nottingham Island in the Hudson Strait in 1904 when her parents were travelling from Arctic Quebec to Baffin Island, Pitseolak spent her earliest years moving with her family among traditional camps near the present-day communities of Iqaluit and Cape Dorset. Shortly after the death of her father, Ottockie, Pitseolak's three brothers arranged a marriage between the teen-aged Pitseolak and a strong young hunter, Ashoona. Pitseolak and Ashoona pursued the traditional migratory lifestyle, often following the caribou in the summertime inland to Nettilling Lake (which is 100 kilometers north of Amadjuak Lake). Through the years, Pitseolak and Ashoona had seventeen children, but only five survived the rigors of Arctic life to adulthood. Ashoona himself died of illness on one of the summer trips to Nettilling Lake, leaving the widowed Pitseolak to care for their still-young family.

Struggling desperately to provide for her children and herself, Pitseolak was grateful for help from her brothers and other hunters. In the late 1950s, Pitseolak moved with her youngest children into Cape Dorset where the new West Baffin Eskimo Co-operative was being formed and where experimental art projects were already enjoying some early success. Responding to encouragement from James Houston and seeing the example of others who had begun to draw, Pitseolak began to make some drawings herself. Her delightfully energetic drawings captured the spirit of traditional life on the land and the vibrancy of her own spirt, and they met an immediate positive response when translated into print images at the West Baffin Eskimo Co-operative. In the

following two-and-a-half decades, Pitseolak Ashoona drew prolifically, executing more than 7,000 drawings depicting her experience of the traditional Inuit culture and expressing her contagious exuberance for life.

Pitseolak Ashoona's images were first published in a Cape Dorset print collection in 1960, and her work appeared in each subsequent collection until her death in 1983. A total of 233 of Pitseolak Ashoona's images were included in Cape Dorset print collections during these twenty-three years. Additionally, Pitseolak Ashoona's work has been featured in more than one hundred group and solo exhibitions of Inuit art including such influential shows as *Cape Dorset—A Decade of Eskimo Prints and Recent Sculpture*, National Gallery of Canada (1967); *Les Eskimos / De Eskimos*, Studio 44, Brussels, Belgium (1974); *Contemporary Eskimo Prints and Sculpture*, Amon Carter Museum of Western Art, Fort Worth, Texas, U.S.A. (1977); *The Inuit Print/L'estampe inuit*, an exhibition organized by the Department of Indian Affairs and Northern Development and the National Museum of Man (now the Canadian Museum of Civilization) that toured internationally (1977-82); *The Coming and Going of the Shaman: Eskimo Shamanism and Art*, Winnipeg Art Gallery (1978); *Inuit Art of the 1970s*, Agnes Etherington Art Centre, Kingston (1979-80); *Grasp Tight the Old Ways: Selections from the Klamer Family Collection of Inuit Art*, Art Gallery of Ontario (1983-85); *Contemporary Inuit Drawings*, Macdonald Stewart Art Centre, Guelph (1987-89); *In the Shadow of the Sun: Contemporary Indian and Inuit Art*, Canadian Museum of Civilization (1988-90); and *Arctic Mirror*, Canadian Museum of Civilization (1990). Her work is also included in numerous private and public collections including the Art Gallery of Ontario; Brown University, Haffenreffer Museum of Anthropology; the Canadian Museum of Civilization; the Laurentian University Museum and Arts Centre; the London Regional Art Gallery; the McMichael Canadian

Art Collection, Kleinburg, the Montréal Museum of Fine Arts; the National Gallery of Canada; the Prince of Wales Northern Heritage Centre, Yellowknife; the Royal Ontario Museum; Simon Fraser University; the University of New Brunswick; the University of Lethbridge; the Vancouver Art Gallery; and the Winnipeg Art Gallery.

In 1971, Pitseolak Ashoona collaborated with Montréal author, Dorothy Harley Eber, to produce a book of drawings and reminiscences entitled *Pitseolak: Pictures out of My Life.* A film by the same name was produced later that same year by the National Film Board of Canada, and two additional films about Pitseolak and her work, *The Way We Live Today* and *Spirits and Monsters* were produced by the International Cinemedia Centre Ltd. in 1975. A retrospective exhibition of drawings by Pitseolak Ashoona organized by the Department of Indian and Northern Affairs in 1975 was accepted by the Smithsonian Institute in Washington as part of Canada's contribution to the United States' bicentennial celebrations.

During her lifetime, Pitseolak was accorded numerous honours for her artistic achievement. These included election to the Royal Canadian Academy of Arts in 1974, a Canada Council Senior Arts Grant in 1975, and the Order of Canada in 1977. Four of Pitseolak's children became artists, including Napachie Pootoogook and three sons who became highly respected sculptors: Qaqaq, Kiugaaq and Komwartok. Pitseolak Ashoona has left a rich legacy of artistic achievement and a lasting example to her children.

facing overleaf:
GAY BIRD (detail)
1967
stonecut and stencil,
proof 1 (edition: 50)
on laid, kozo paper

printed by *Eegyvudluk Pootoogook*, 1931–
44 x 62.3 cm
Cape Dorset 1967,
no. 10

Memories of Pitseolak Ashoona

Photo by / Gift of Norman E. Hallendy,
McMichael Canadian Art Collection Archives

By Napachie Pootoogook, her daughter
My mother's way of life was taught to us children. She would feed us and clothe us even though we had no father. Life was very difficult for my mother, trying to raise us while some of our relatives had easier lives. She made drawings to support us, and she encouraged me to do the same. She has passed away recently.

She tried very hard to clothe and feed us, and later on in her life she didn't go through too much hard times. I thank her very much still, even though she's gone now and the memory of her is precious. My mother weathered it all even though there were some very difficult times for years. She died with her children respecting her.
(Written March 1991)

She used to use her own imagination and she didn't like intrusion when she was doing her work because she didn't want her train of thought to be disturbed. She used to do her work in her bedroom in order not to be distracted. She didn't say, 'I am going to be making it this way,' she used her own imagination.

The memories I have about my mother's struggles are very vivid in my mind and I sometimes wish that she was still alive so that I might have the opportunity to return the help she gave to us, since she helped us a great deal. At that time, too, it was a very cold climate with meagre means of fueling the lamps to make the place warm. That is my emotional tie with my mother.

She kept on giving of herself right up to her death. I find a special joy about that.

At the time she started to travel to the South, I find joy in knowing that she was treated well and that her hard-earned efforts were [rewarded]. I was happy in knowing that she was allowed to do something she enjoyed.
(1991 interview with Odette Leroux)

By Kenojuak Ashevak

I will now go on to tell a story about Pitseolak Ashoona's drawings. She would draw scenes of hunters with their backpacks, and of people standing outside by the igloo with dogs in the scene. And as an artist, there are times when nothing will come to you to make a drawing of, and there would be times when she'd just start laughing. As I would visit with her, she made a lot of different drawings as well as carvings. I would always be amazed at her abilities as I watched her. Those are what I remember the most about her.

I would always enjoy going over to Pitseolak's. We would always play some games when I was a young girl. She always made me feel welcome. We would play some games and dance around, she gave me dancing lessons when I went over and I would try my hardest to learn. Sometimes she would play her accordion. Her only daughter, Napachie, also got very attached to me. Napachie Pootoogook would refuse to let me go as she was an only girl there.

(Written March 1991)

By Pitaloosie Saila

I will write about the time I started remembering Pitseolak Ashoona. It was when we lived in a camp called Keatuk not far from Cape Dorset. She and her children lived there among her relatives.

She was known as a friendly, kind person to everybody. She used to be loved by girls and boys, even the adults used to be fond of her. She always seemed to show affection towards them. She used to laugh quite often and tell about stories she

knew and experienced from long ago; stories of excitement, of laughter and those of sad times. Not only her own but also those of others, many ways of how Inuit lived, ways she herself experienced about how the real Inuit lived long ago.

The stories she used to tell of those days I still remember to this day and will not forget them.

(Written February 1992)

UNTITLED
1962
engraving, proof
(edition: 50)
on wove, rag paper
31.5 x 45.7 cm
Cape Dorset 1962,
no. 31

I became an artist to earn money but I think I am a real artist…. I draw the things I have never seen, the monsters and spirits, and I draw the old ways, the things we did long ago before there were many white men. I don't know how many draw-ings I have done but more than a thousand. There are many Pitseolaks now—I have signed my name many times.
Quote by Pitseolak Ashoona from Dorothy Harley Eber's book, *Pitseolak: Pictures out of My Life.*

HAPPY FAMILY
1963
engraving, proof 1
(edition: 50)
on wove, rag paper
31.9 x 45.2 cm
Cape Dorset 1963,
no. 16

*When James Houston,
whom we call Sowmik
[Saumik]—the left-
handed one—came to
Cape Dorset and told
me to draw the old
ways, I began to put
the old costumes into
the drawings and
prints.*
Quote by Pitseolak Ashoona
from Dorothy Harley Eber's
book, *Pitseolak: Pictures out of
My Life.*

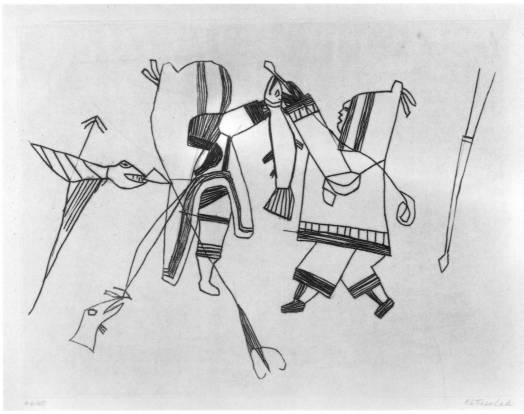

UNTITLED
1962
engraving, 26/50
on wove, rag paper
31.7 x 45.3 cm
Cape Dorset 1962,
no. 55

FURRY OWL
1963
engraving, proof II
(edition: 50)
on wove, rag paper
31.6 x 45.5 cm
Cape Dorset 1963,
no. 18

WITCH AND FRIENDS
1963
(Original title: *Witch
with Friends*)
engraving, 17/50
on wove, rag paper
36.1 x 41.7 cm
Cape Dorset 1963,
no. 19

TATTOOED WOMAN
1963
stonecut, proof III
(edition: 50)
on wove paper
printed by *Lukta
Qiatsuk, 1928–*
65.9 x 62 cm
Cape Dorset 1963,
no. 22

*Many of the women
had tattoo marks on
their faces and my
mother had them, too.
They used to do it with
a needle and caribou
thread soaked in oil
and soot from the
'kudlik'— the seal-oil
lamp. They used to
pull the thread through
the skin and the skin
would be swollen for*
*many days. I don't
know exactly why peo-
ple had tattoos but I
believe the women did
it because they
thought it was pretty. I
did, too. When I was
young I tried a few
marks on my arm, as
you can see.*
Quote by Pitseolak Ashoona
from Dorothy Harley Eber's
book, *Pitseolak: Pictures out of
My Life.*

PEOPLE
1964
engraving, proof IV
(edition: 50)
on laid, kozo paper
25 x 30 cm
Cape Dorset 1964–65,
no. 19

CROSSING THE RIVER
1967
stonecut, proof
(edition: 50)
on laid, kozo paper
printed by *Iyola
Kingwatsiak* 1933–
43.7 x 62.6 cm
Cape Dorset 1967,
no. 9

*We made all these
travels in a sealskin
boat. Such boats had
wooden frames that
were covered with
skins. They used to be
called the women's
boats because they
were sewn by the
women. Many women
sewed to make one
boat. Some boats had
sails made from the
intestine of the whale,
but we had no sail and
we had no motors
then.*

Quote by Pitseolak Ashoona
from Dorothy Harley Eber's
book, *Pitseolak: Pictures out of
My Life.*

GAY BIRD
1967
stonecut and stencil,
proof 1 (edition: 50)
on laid, kozo paper
printed by *Eegyvudluk
Pootoogook*, 1931–
44 x 62.3 cm
Cape Dorset 1967,
no. 10

Woman and Dogs
1967
engraving, proof 1
(edition: 50)
on wove, rag paper
33 x 25.2 cm
Cape Dorset 1967,
no. 67

Woman with Geese
1966
engraving, proof 1
(edition: 50)
on wove, rag paper
33.2 x 50 cm
Cape Dorset 1967,
no. 71

When I was a little girl my father and mother taught me how to catch a goose. Four people would corner a goose and then my parents would tell me to run up behind it, hooting and shouting, and put my foot on its neck. I'd run and I'd catch the goose and I'd stand there waving my arms like a bird. Sometimes we'd all have headaches from shouting and yelling.
Quote by Pitseolak Ashoona from Dorothy Harley Eber's book, *Pitseolak: Pictures out of My Life.*

EVE AND THE
SERPENT
1968
stonecut, proof II
(edition: 50)
on laid, kozo paper
printed by *Iyola
Kingwatsiak*, 1933–
62.8 x 43.6 cm
Cape Dorset 1968,
no. 38

INUKSHUK BUILDERS
1967
stonecut, proof II
(edition: 50)
on laid, kozo paper
printed by *Lukta
Qiatsuk, 1928–*
61.9 x 70 cm
Cape Dorset 1968,
no. 40

*Sometimes, when we
camped in a place for
the first time, we would
put up an 'inukshuk'.*
Quote by Pitseolak Ashoona
from Dorothy Harley Eber's
book, *Pitseolak: Pictures out of
My Life.*

Women juggling stones   LI. Cape 67   proof II   Pitseolak

WOMEN JUGGLING
STONES
1967
stonecut, proof II
(edition: 50)
on laid, kozo paper
printed by *Lukta
Qiatsuk, 1928–*
31.3 x 43.1 cm
Cape Dorset 1968,
no. 42

*Ashoona used to like
to juggle. He could
keep three small stones
in the air and some-
times, just for two sec-
onds, I could keep
three stones up there,
too.*
Quote by Pitseolak Ashoona
from Dorothy Harley Eber's
book, *Pitseolak: Pictures out of
My Life.*

SUMMER TENT OF OLD
1969
stonecut, proof II
(edition: 50)
on wove, kozo paper
printed by *Eegyvudluk
Pootoogook, 1931–*
59.4 x 82.5 cm
Cape Dorset 1969, no. 8

*The sealskin tent was
changed every summer
because it would dry
out and then it was
very hard to use. I used
to see my mother
make these tents. She
would scrape the* udjuk
[ujjuk] *three times with
the* ulu *and sew the
skins on the ground.
These skins could dry
out very quickly, too,
so, damp moss would
be brought from the
tundra to cover them
as she worked.*

Quote by Pitseolak Ashoona
from Dorothy Harley Eber's
book, *Pitseolak: Pictures out of
My Life*.

Stone block carved for
SUMMER TENT OF OLD
1969
grey stone
42.5 x 77 x 3.2 cm
IV-C-4006

BIRD WITH AVATAQ
1970
(Original title: *Bird
with Arialuk*)
stonecut, proof III
(edition: 50)
on wove, kozo paper
printed by *Eegyvudluk
Pootoogook*, 1931–
50.3 x 62.8 cm
Cape Dorset 1971,
no. 13

BEAR ATTACKING SEAL
1973
stonecut, proof II
(edition: 50)
on laid, kozo paper
printed by *Lukta
Qiatsuk*, 1928–
63.1 x 43.2 cm
Cape Dorset 1973,
no. 14

OUR CAMP
1974
stonecut, proof
(edition: 50)
on laid, kozo paper
printed by *Saggiaktok
Saggiaktok*, 1932–
86 x 63.5 cm
Cape Dorset 1974,
no. 17

*The text [written on
the original] drawing
reads: 'THESE PEOPLE
HAVE GONE OUT
hunting for animals
and have caught fish.
They are sleeping in a
partially pitched tent
as they are just out
hunting.'*
Blodgett, Jean. *In Cape Dorset
We Do It This Way: Three
Decades of Inuit Printmaking.*
Kleinburg, Ontario: McMichael
Canadian Art Collection,
1991, p. 82

Our Camp   Stone Cut   Proof   Dorset 1974   Pitseolak

OLD WOMEN
SPEAK OF OWL
1974
stonecut, proof 1
(edition: 50)
on wove, kozo paper
printed by *Qabaroak
Qatsiya*, 1942–
86.4 x 62.8 cm
Cape Dorset 1974,
no. 19

Woman
with Goslings
1974
stonecut, proof 1
(edition: 50)
on laid, kozo paper
printed by *Lukta
Qiatsuk*, 1928–
62.7 x 43.1 cm
Cape Dorset 1974,
no. 9

First Bird of Spring   *Lithograph*   Proof I   Edition 50   Ikuhaki

FIRST BIRD OF SPRING
1975
lithograph, proof 1
(edition: 31)
on wove, rag paper
watermark: BFK Rives/
France
printed by *Qiatsuq
Niviaqsi*, 1941– and
Pee Mikkigak 1940–
75.9 x 56.2 cm
Cape Dorset 1975,
no. 51

FAMILY CAMPING
IN TUNIIT RUINS
1976
(Original title: *Family
Camping in Tuniq
Ruins*)
stonecut and stencil,
proof (edition: 50)
on laid, kozo paper
printed by *Qabaroak
Qatsiya*, 1942–
86 x 63 cm
Cape Dorset 1976, no. 5

CRYING CHILD
1979
lithograph, 40/50
on wove, rag paper
printed by *Aoudla
Pudlat*, 1951–
28.5 x 20.8 cm
Cape Dorset 1979,
no. L21

THE SHAMAN'S WIFE
1980
stonecut and stencil,
proof III (edition: 50)
on laid, kozo paper
printed by *Pee
Mikkigak*, 1940–
71.8 x 51 cm
Cape Dorset 1980,
no. 42

*The shaman.… They
were Eskimos [Inuit]
just like other people
but they had these
strange powers. They
had power over the
hunt—they could bring
the animals—and they
had power to kill.…
They were good
shamans and bad
shamans but most peo-
ple feared them.*
Quote by Pitseolak Ashoona
from Dorothy Harley Eber's
book, *Pitseolak: Pictures out of
My Life.*

To Rescue a
Drowning Hunter
1983
lithograph, 15/50
on wove, rag paper
watermark: BFK
Rives/France
printed by *Pitseolak
Niviaqsi*, 1947–
65.5 x 51 cm
Cape Dorset 1984,
no. 8 (uncatalogued)
Portfolio II

To Rescue a Drowning Man   Lithograph 15/50   Dorset 1983   Pitseolak ᐱᑦᓯᐅᓛ

ONE CAPTIVE BIRD
1983
stonecut and stencil,
45/50
on wove, kozo paper
printed by *Eegyvudluk
Pootoogook*, 1931–
43 x 53 cm
Cape Dorset 1983,
no. 33

MIGRATION TOWARDS
OUR SUMMER CAMP
1983
lithograph, 15/50
on wove, rag paper
watermark: BFK
Rives/France
printed by *Pitseolak
Niviaqsi*, 1947–
66.2 x 51.1 cm
Cape Dorset 1984, no. 7
(uncatalogued)
Portfolio II

*Both in summer and
winter we used to move
a lot. In summer there
were always very big
mosquitoes. I have
made many drawings
of moving camp in
summertime and I
always put in the mos-
quitoes. I do not like
insects.*

Quote by Pitseolak Ashoona
from Dorothy Harley Eber's
book, *Pitseolak: Pictures out of
My Life.*

MANY-WINGED BIRD
1983
stonecut and stencil,
49/50
on laid, kozo paper
printed by *Arnasu
Qajurajuk*, 1940–
56.5 x 65.5 cm
Cape Dorset 1983,
no. 28

Lucy Qinnuayuak

The time I am happiest about my drawing
is when I see a person who likes my drawings
and when the person tells me
that she or he likes my drawings.

1979 Cape Dorset Print Catalogue

Lucy Qinnuayuak
1915–1982

As is the case with many South Baffin Inuit families, Lucy Qinnuayuak's family has strong ties with Arctic Quebec. Lucy herself was born in Salluit, Northern Quebec, in 1915 and moved to Baffin Island as a young child. Approximately a year after the death of Lucy's father in about 1919, Lucy's widowed mother, Sanaaq, travelled to Baffin Island with her young family aboard the Hudson's Bay Company supply ship, *Nascopie*, hoping to rejoin relatives who could help her and her young children. There Lucy's mother married Takata Meesa, and Lucy spent her childhood travelling with her mother and stepfather among the camps in the area of Cape Dorset. As a teenager, Lucy married Tikitu Qinnuayuak in an arranged marriage that was blessed by a missionary in a group ceremony aboard the *Nascopie*. Lucy and Tikitu continued to follow the traditional hunting lifestyle, moving about the Foxe Peninsula and living at various camps, primarily Shapujuak, Ittiliakjuk, Igalallik, and Kangia.

While living at Kangia in the 1950s, Lucy and her brother-in-law, Niviaqsi, were among the first to respond to James Houston's request for drawings. Admitting that she was shy about her drawings at first, Lucy welcomed the opportunity to earn some income from her works. This was to become particularly important to Lucy in 1961 when her husband was evacuated to the South for tuberculosis, and her ability to earn an income on her own became critical. Tikitu responded positively to treatment and returned a year later, but they remained permanently in Cape Dorset after that time. Lucy and Tikitu had nine children, five

of whom died in childhood, and adopted two others, one of whom was their grandson; they also took into their care the five orphaned children of Tikitu's brother, Niviaqsi, following the death of Niviaqsi in 1959 and the death of Niviaqsi's wife a few years later.

In the final two decades of her life, Lucy drew prolifically, creating thousands of fanciful images of wide-eyed birds and scenes depicting women's roles in the traditional Inuit culture. Lucy worked primarily in graphite pencil and coloured pencil but did some experimenting during the 1970s and 1980s with broad washes of watercolour and acrylic paints which she received first from Terry Ryan [at the West Baffin Eskimo Co-operative] and later from visiting Toronto artist, Kate Graham. Her husband, Tikitu, was also involved in the arts, making occasional sculptures and later drawings, and Lucy's niece, Kenojuak Ashevak, became increasingly prominent for her artistic accomplishments.

Lucy's spirited images were first included in the Cape Dorset print collection in 1961 and missed only one annual collection between 1961 and the time of her death in 1982. She had a total of 136 prints published in twenty-one Cape Dorset print collections. Some of Lucy's earliest images were also adapted for textile Christmas card designs as part of some early experimental fabric printing efforts in Cape Dorset. One of her images was selected for a UNICEF greeting card in 1972, and another for a banner for the Summer Olympics in 1976. The 1971 and 1983 Cape Dorset calendars were devoted entirely to works by Lucy Qinnuayuak.

Through the years, Lucy Qinnuayuak's graphic images have been exhibited in more than eighty group and solo shows. These have included *The Inuit Print/L'estampe inuit*, an exhibition organized by the Department of Indian Affairs and the National Museum of Man (now the Canadian Museum of Civilization) that toured internationally (1977-82); *Looking South*, Winnipeg Art Gallery

(1978); *Inuit Art in the 1970s*, Agnes Etherington Art Centre (1979-80); *Grasp Tight the Old Ways: Selections from the Klamer Family Collection of Inuit Art*, Art Gallery of Ontario (1983-85); *The Arctic/L'artique*, UNESCO, Paris, France (1983); *Arctic Vision: Art of the Canadian Inuit*, touring exhibition organized by the Department of Indian Affairs and Northern Development and Canadian Arctic Producers (1984-86); and *Flights of Fancy—Kenojuak Ashevak, Lucy Qinnuayuak, Pitaloosie Saila*, Art Gallery of Ontario (1989-91).

Examples of Lucy Qinnuayuak's art are included in numerous collections including the Art Gallery of Ontario; the Canadian Museum of Civilization; the Inuit Cultural Institute, Rankin Inlet; the Laurentian University Museum and Arts Centre; the London Regional Art Gallery; the Macdonald Stewart Art Centre, Guelph; the Mendel Art Gallery, Saskatoon; the National Gallery of Canada; the New Brunswick Museum; the Prince of Wales Northern Heritage Centre, Yellowknife; the Royal Ontario Museum; the Winnipeg Art Gallery; and York University. The stone for her 1961 print, *Large Bear*, was donated to the Tate Gallery, London, by Sir Charles Gimpel and is on display at the Scott Polar Research Institute, Cambridge, England.

Lucy Qinnuayuak Remembers

Photo by Tessa Macintosh,
circa 1975.

When we were living down at Qungia [Kangia], my husband came here to Cape Dorset to get supplies, and Saumik [Houston] gave him a paper to take back for me to draw on. He did that, and I started drawing on my own. Saumik wasn't at the camp. My husband would come here to Cape Dorset for supplies, and he would bring my drawings, too. Saumik would give another piece of paper for me to draw on. My husband would go back to Qungia, and when he could come for more supplies, he would take the drawings to Saumik and bring back more papers. Saumik would give money for the drawings.
(1979 Cape Dorset Print Catalogue)

When I started drawing, I would draw but if I heard somebody coming into my tent, I would just put my drawings away, because I was shy of someone making fun of my drawings or something…. I didn't realize that they would be shown to other people when I did them the first time.
(1979 Cape Dorset Print Catalogue)

A lot of people really like my drawings even though I find drawing so difficult. When I heard that people like my drawings, I can really feel it inside me—it pleases me. When I drew these pictures, they didn't make any sense, but now that they are printed they look more sensible. I am happy. A lot of people in the South have never seen me, but they know me by my drawings. I find it very hard thinking what I am going to draw, although it seems so easy. When James and Alma Houston were still in Cape Dorset they asked me to draw, and that's when I first started. In those days we still lived in camp.
(1978 Cape Dorset Print Catalogue)

I never make my drawings balance on both sides even though I try to. After I finish them, I see that they are only a little bit balanced.
(1978 Cape Dorset Print Catalogue)

73

Kenojuak Ashevak remembers Lucy Qinnuayuak:

I will now talk about my aunt Lucy, who was also an artist. I remember she always drew geese, more so than anything else. I remember she always enjoyed drawing especially geese. I would also babysit my aunt's children.

(Written March 1991)

FAMILY OF BIRDS
1963
stonecut, 10/50
on wove, kozo paper
printed by *Lukta Qiatsuk*, 1928–
61.9 x 88 cm
Cape Dorset 1963,
no. 66

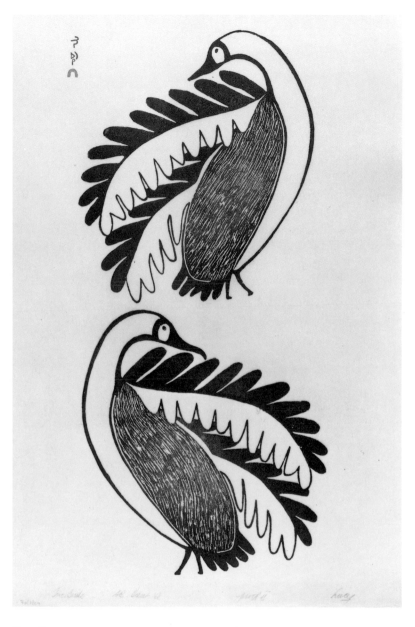

Stone block
carved for Two Birds
1968
dark green stone
68.5 x 29.5 x 3 cm
IV-C-4005

Two Birds
1968
stonecut, proof II
(edition: 50)
on laid, kozo paper
printed by *Timothy
Ottochie*, 1904–82
62.5 x 43.1 cm
Cape Dorset 1968,
no. 15

Spectator Bird   Dorset 1969   proof III   Kiaq.

SPECTATOR BIRDS
1969
stonecut, proof III
(edition: 50)
on laid, kozo paper
printed by *Lukta*
Qiatsuk, 1928–
43.5 x 62.7 cm
Cape Dorset 1970,
no. 29

SPRING CAMP
1969
stonecut, proof II
(edition: 50)
on laid, kozo paper
printed by *Iyola
Kingwatsiak*, 1933–
62.5 x 85.5 cm
Cape Dorset 1970,
no. 31

UMIAK, KAYAK AND
BIRDS
circa 1972
felt pen
on wove, bleached-
wood-pulp paper
45.5 x 61 cm
signed
Gift of Alma Houston,
Lunenburg, Nova Scotia,
1979
IV-C-4797

DANCERS AND
GRAMOPHONE
circa 1972
felt pen
on wove, bleached-wood-
pulp paper
45.7 x 61.2 cm
signed
Gift of Alma Houston,
Lunenburg, Nova Scotia,
1979
IV-C-4799

COMPOSITION
1972
stonecut, proof II
(edition: 50)
on laid, kozo paper
printed by *Timothy
Ottochie*, 1904–82
61.8 x 85.1 cm
Cape Dorset 1972,
no. 1

CAMP SCENE
circa 1972
felt pen and graphite
on wove, bleached-wood-
pulp paper
45.6 x 60.9 cm
signed
Gift of Alma Houston,
Lunenburg, Nova Scotia,
1979
IV-C-4798

TWO WOMEN PLAYING
1977
felt pen, crayon and
acrylic
on wove, rag paper
52.5 x 66.2 cm
signed
Anonymous donor, 1986
Collection of the
University of Lethbridge
Art Gallery, Lethbridge,
Alberta
986.734

*In those days, the
women would get
together and play at
juggling, and they
would try to beat each
other. They would see
who could juggle for
the longest time, and
then there would be a
winner. Thinking of
that and of the old
ways made me draw....*

*It reminds me of happy
time and what women
did in those days. Even
the men used to play
that game.*
1978 Cape Dorset Print
Catalogue

WOMEN
AND CHILDREN
circa 1973
felt pen
on wove, bleached-wood-
pulp paper
45.5 x 61 cm
signed
Gift of Alma Houston,
Lunenburg, Nova Scotia,
1979
IV-C-4800

SPIRIT BOAT
1972
stonecut, proof II
(edition: 50)
on laid, kozo paper
printed by *Timothy
Ottochie*, 1904–82
40.1 x 62.4 cm
Cape Dorset 1972,
no. 2

*I have never seen a
spirit, but I heard a
man telling stories of
them on the radio.*
1978 Cape Dorset Print
Catalogue

WOMEN
CARRYING FISH
1972
stonecut, 47/50
on laid, kozo paper
printed by *Timothy
Ottochie*, 1904–82
41.8 x 61.3 cm
Cape Dorset 1972,
no. 4

WOMEN AND OWLS
1977
crayon and felt pen
on wove, rag paper
51.8 x 65.8 cm
signed
Anonymous donor, 1986
Collection of the
University of Lethbridge
Art Gallery, Lethbridge,
Alberta
986.735

HUNTERS,
BEARS AND SEALS
1977
felt pen, crayon and
acrylic
on wove, rag paper
55.9 x 75.7 cm
signed
Anonymous donor, 1986
Collection of the
University of Lethbridge
Art Gallery, Lethbridge,
Alberta
986.781

*I put the polar bear in
this picture... because I
heard that somebody
really liked another
drawing of a polar bear
that I made.*
1978 Cape Dorset Print
Catalogue

CAMP SCENE WITH
ANIMALS AND BIRDS
1977
felt pen, crayon, chalk
and acrylic
on wove, rag paper
55 x 74.1 cm
signed
Anonymous donor, 1986
Collection of the
University of Lethbridge
Art Gallery, Lethbridge,
Alberta
986.784

FISH WEIR
1977
felt pen, crayon and
acrylic
on wove, rag paper
55.8 x 75.4 cm
signed
Anonymous donor, 1986
Collection of the
University of Lethbridge
Art Gallery, Lethbridge,
Alberta
786.782

FANTASY BIRDS
1977
felt pen, crayon and
acrylic
on wove, rag paper
56.1 x 76.2 cm
signed
Anonymous donor, 1986
Collection of the
University of Lethbridge
Art Gallery, Lethbridge,
Alberta
986.785

TULUKARA
(YOUNG RAVEN)
1977
stonecut and stencil,
33/50
on laid, kozo paper
printed by *Timothy
Ottochie*, 1904–82
59.5 x 62.7 cm
Cape Dorset 1977,
no. 38

PILATUKTU
(SKINNING THE SEAL)
1979
stonecut and stencil,
proof (edition: 50)
on laid, kozo paper
printed by *Laisa
Qajurajuk*, 1935–
46.5 x 61.5 cm
Cape Dorset 1979,
no. 31

A DISPLAY
OF FEATHERS
1982
stonecut and stencil,
43/50
on laid, kozo paper
printed by *Timothy
Ottochie*, 1904–82
42.5 x 76.5 cm
Cape Dorset 1982,
no. 30

Recollections
1983
lithograph, 8/25
on wove, rag paper
watermark: BFK
Rives/France
printed by *Pootoogook
Qiatsuq*, 1959–
66.4 x 102 cm
Cape Dorset 1983,
no. L23

Kenojuak Ashevak

I like that one because it portrays a landscape and sea
with some hills during the spring season.
I always enjoy that season because it is
when migratory birds start to come in.

Comment written by Kenojuak in
March 1991 about one of her
favourite prints

Kenojuak Ashevak
1927–

An extremely talented artist and one of the first women to engage herself in the new arts projects in the late 1950s, Kenojuak has been a sculptor and graphic artist for more than 30 years and is today one of the most widely recognized living Inuit artists. Like almost all Inuit of her generation, Kenojuak Ashevak spent her early years living on the land following the traditional Inuit lifestyle. She was born at Ikirashaq and grew up travelling from camp to camp on South Baffin Island and, for a short period, in Arctic Quebec. As a very young woman, Kenojuak was married to Johnniebo Ashevak and lived with him in various camps including Qarmaajuk, Kangia, and Peter Pitseolak's camp, Keatuk.

While in her twenties, Kenojuak suffered from tuberculosis and spent nearly four years in a hospital in Québec. During this time, her two eldest children died from eating rotted walrus meat, and her youngest child died during an influenza epidemic. Upon her recovery, she rejoined her husband and resumed the traditional Inuit camp life. In the late 1950s at Keatuk, Kenojuak and Johnniebo, encouraged by James Houston, began to carve and draw. Kenojuak's print image, *Rabbit Eating Seaweed*, which was inspired by a silhouette pattern she had done earlier on a skin pouch, was included in the first catalogued print collection to be issued from Cape Dorset in 1959, and she has been one of the most active contributors to the annual collections since that time. Kenojuak and Johnniebo moved to Cape Dorset in 1966 so their children could attend school, and they continued to work closely together until Johnniebo's death in 1972.

Kenojuak has had a total of 188 images published in thirty of the thirty-five Cape Dorset print collections issued since 1959, and she has also executed a number of important commissioned works including a ninety-six-foot plaster mural which she and Johnniebo created collaboratively for the Canadian Pavilion at Expo '70 in Osaka, Japan. Other prominent commissions include a print for the World Wildlife Fund print portfolio in 1977, a 1990 lithograph, *Nunavut Qajanartuk (Our Beautiful Land)*, a limited edition of only three commissioned by the Department of Indian Affairs and Northern Development to commemorate the 1990 signing of the Inuit land claims Agreement-in-Principle by the Tungavik Federation of Nunavut and the Government of Canada, and a 1992 special commission to produce the piece called *Nunavut (Our Land)*, which was also produced in a limited edition of only three to commemorate the 1993 signing ceremony for the Tungavik Federation of Nunavut Settlement Agreement in Iqaluit.

Works by Kenojuak Ashevak have appeared in almost every major group exhibition of Inuit art in the past thirty years, and she has more than one hundred exhibitions to her credit including such landmark exhibitions as *Sculpture/Inuit: Masterworks of the Canadian Arctic*, the exhibition organized by the Canadian Eskimo Arts Council (1971-73) that toured internationally; *The Inuit Print/L'estampe inuit*, the exhibition organized by the Department of Indian Affairs and Northern Development and the National Museum of Man (now the Canadian Museum of Civilization) that toured internationally (1977-1982); *Grasp Tight the Old Ways: Selections from the Klamer Family Collection of Inuit Art*, Art Gallery of Ontario (1983-85); *The Swinton Collection of Inuit Art*, Winnipeg Art Gallery (1987); *Contemporary Inuit Drawings*, Macdonald Stewart Art Centre, Guelph (1987-89); *In the Shadow of the Sun: Contemporary Indian and Inuit Art*, Canadian Museum of Civilization (1988-90); and *Arctic Mirror*, Canadian Museum of

Civilization (1990). Kenojuak Ashevak's work is included in dozens of private and public collections including the Canadian Museum of Civilization; the McMichael Canadian Art Collection; the Montréal Museum of Fine Arts; the National Gallery of Canada; Northwestern Michigan College, Dennos Museum; the Royal Ontario Museum; the University of Guelph; the Vancouver Art Gallery; the Victoria and Albert Museum; and the Winnipeg Art Gallery.

Kenojuak Ashevak was featured in a film, *The Living Stone*, produced by the National Film Board in 1962 and is the only Inuit artist to date to be featured in a book-length historical and interpretive monograph, Jean Blodgett's *Kenojuak*, published in 1985. Kenojuak's images enjoy widespread familiarity as her 1960 print, *Enchanted Owl*, was reproduced on a Canadian postage stamp commemorating the centennial of the Northwest Territories in 1970, and her 1961 print, *Return of the Sun*, was chosen for a seventeen-cent stamp in 1980. Through the years, Kenojuak Ashevak has received a number of honours recognizing her outstanding artistic achievement; these tributes include the Order of Canada in 1967, election to the Royal Canadian Academy of Arts in 1974, appointment as Companion to the Order of Canada in 1982, an Honourary Doctorate from Queens University in 1991, and an Honourary Doctor of Laws from the University of Toronto in 1992. Kenojuak Ashevak continues to be very active in the arts and is currently exploring new themes and stylistic possibilities which promise to take her work in new directions in the future.

facing overleaf:
TIMIATJUAK
(LARGE BIRDS)
1987
lithograph, 46/50
on wove, rag paper

printed by *Pootoogook Qiatsuq*, 1959–
50.5 x 65.5 cm
Cape Dorset 1987,
no. 15

Kenojuak's Memories

Kenojuak Ashevak

I WILL TELL about the time of my birth. I remember trying to get out towards the light I could see. But every time I tried the pathway, something prevented me and I would go back. Finally I made it out, but when I did it was so bright and cold. There were Kakkaluk and Nasaluk when I went out. I saw huge people, and huge hands picked me up. And as I was picked up I don't remember anything else, but I remember starting to cry. I remember I wanted to get away from them but I could not. Apparently I fell asleep then so I have no other recollection after that about being born.

I'll write down what I remember distinctly from my early childhood. [When I was two years old,] we were headed for Ivujivik and I was at the bottom of the canoe. I remember I was observing and listening to everything. I would watch my father and mother and my uncles while we travelled towards the Qikiqtarjuaq Inlet which is called Anaulirvik, near Ivujivik. That seems to be where my memories began when I was only a year old, and from there I fell asleep in the canoe.

Something else that I remember from my childhood. Although I was only a child, I must have gone through traumatic times. What had happened was that my father's brothers had died in a boat accident. Perhaps I remember this because I was feeling for my cousins. What I had heard was that the ice had broken away from the main ice. I remember my mother and father weeping. And from there my memory fades again, like I had fallen asleep. Those are the early memories that I have.

Another memory that I have is at the same year I was two years old, during the wintertime while we lived at Pujjunaq, near Akuliviq. It was that year my father was killed. My brother and sister and I were in bed. After my mother was outside, I remember my father was crying as [he] was telling us not to cry. He told us these things just before he was killed. There was shouting and anger at that time, and he was killed. After he died, I wanted to be shown his blood, and I was shown his blood as I would not accept his death otherwise. He was lying in a pool of blood, dead. That had a huge impact on my life though I was a very young child. And from there, my memory fades. That memory is one of the hardships I had to deal with.

And I remember the time when we returned to Ivujivik from Pujjunaq. Then we travelled from Ivujivik to Kagisualaak, a Hudson's Bay Company post near Ivujivik and from there across to Cape Dorset by the ship called *Nascopie*. When we arrived at Cape Dorset, I remember feeling we had landed among a completely different group of Inuit. But when my aunt (my father's sister) saw me, she started to cry as she hugged me, and then she and my mother wept together. That must also have been traumatic for me because I remember it so well. I have gone through a lot of hardship. And even though I was so young a child and without a father at that time, I was never mistreated.

Then as we were travelling from Cape Dorset to Shapujuak to where my grandmother lived, I thought that we would come across total strangers again. But it turned out that my relatives walked from Cape Dorset to Shapujuak. They were Tikitu, Etidloui, Tigularaq, and my mother; also my brother, Adamie Alariaq, and my sister, Qimmikpikuluk Ukkuttaq. All my relatives were there except my youngest brother, Attachie, who was adopted to another family as soon as we arrived in Cape Dorset. When we were walking to Shapujuak, I remember the Inuit were being counted. As I rode on Etidloui's backpack I would occasionally fall asleep. I also remember one of my youngest uncles was riding atop of Tikitu's backpack but would walk once in a while. Whenever they stopped to rest, he and I would spend some time playing.

Now, I'll go on to tell about my older sister, Qimmikpikuluk Ukkuttaq and myself travelling during the springtime to go get my grandmother while she was still living at Shapujuak. While my uncles were travelling by canoe, my sister and I were travelling by dog team and I remember I really enjoyed it. As my sister could not get the dogs to turn, I would get them to make a turn to where I wanted them to go. We were both very young at that time when we were given the responsibility of getting the dog team to go to our destination. But when we arrived at the camp and were acknowledged for doing what we did, we ran into my grandmother's tent to hide. Then as we left camp again, we were aided on the dog team by two men, as my older sister could not handle the dogs even though I was able to command them to turn where they should.

Now I'll move on to the time I was a teenager, when one of my uncles and I were being trained to drive a dog team. I was watching the dogs to keep them still while my uncle was stalking a bearded seal. And as I was unable to keep the dogs from charging when my uncle was preparing to shoot, I was blamed for the loss of the seal and got soaking wet in the process. His dogs got all excited when their master fired his gun, and only when they heard the gun shot would they be allowed to follow. I remember feeling sad if I couldn't go along seal hunting, and when I would be allowed I would be so excited. I never did like having to keep the dogs quiet while my uncle was stalking a seal.

Now I would like to talk about hunting. Three of us were out caribou hunting on a skidoo, and it was about the first time I saw caribou. That was when caribou would come this close around here. There was myself, my brother, his wife Nakashuk, and their young son, Adamie. My brother and his wife left to go after the caribou on foot, leaving the sled and their son behind. As it turned out the caribou headed straight for the sled, so [Adamie] lay down beside the sled because he was so afraid. Later when we got back together to skin the caribou that was caught, three more caribou showed up very close to where we were. Nakashuk and her husband started shooting at them while I stood by. Then my brother asked me why I hadn't reached for a rifle yet, so I picked one up and started shooting as well. I remember being so happy then.

Another story I would like to tell is when my stepmother. Osuituk, and I went by dog team to Qanippanik, a Hudson's Bay Company post near Ivujivik, to go get our cache. We were so proud of ourselves to be doing that because my companion had a small baby in her *amauti*. She went to check the traps as well. Then, as we headed back home, I remembered the harpoon tip that had been left behind at Shapujuak. As we were travelling by dog team and my stepmother could not take charge of the dogs, it was left up to me again to make them change their direction. When I got the dogs to change direction, they started speeding towards the shore line. Our lead dog bit a seal, but it still got away even though the dog tried to hang on to it. We just ended up laughing about it even though we were sad we had lost it. As it was springtime, the men were canoeing while we used the dog team. It was beautiful to live that way then, but even then I never did like having to keep the dogs quiet as someone else stalked a seal. I am telling about my memories as a young teenager.

I would like to continue telling a story about my life. I used to be so embarrassed to be a left-handed person. If there was a group of people, there was no way I would use an *ulu* to cut a piece of meat. My grandfather used to be left-handed too, I remember, and he would try and discourage me from using my left hand because he knew what he had gone through. He would even tie up one of my sleeves so I could not use that hand. In those days it used to be embarrassing to be left-handed; it's not that way today. I wouldn't have any trouble to get my left arm out to use it even if it were tied up. Perhaps it's because of my old age that I don't find it embarrassing any more to be left-handed. That is one of the experiences I had to go through that was hard on me.

I'll now talk about the time my husband, Johnniebo, and I

GODDESS OF THE SKY
1980
stonecut and stencil, proof III (edition: 50) on laid, kozo paper printed by *Simigak Simeonie*, 1939–
60.5 x 73.4 cm
Cape Dorset 1980, no. 11

This is an image of an Inuk, the face of an Inuk, these are her hairs. These two [braids] made this way are not darkened but they are to make the face more appealing and that one. These are coloured to make her more womanly. These two are birds and these two are sea mammals

with fore flippers. The way they are made is just from my imagination. I am always adding something to make the picture more fascinating when I am not really making anything that is real.
1992 interview with Marion E. Jackson and Odette Leroux

went to Ottawa with our three children. Once we reached there we were provided with an Inuk interpreter. I went to Ottawa that time to make a drawing that would be sent to Japan. Where we stayed and worked was air conditioned so we enjoyed our stay. Another time I was sent to Ottawa to get my eyes checked. I was afraid even though my husband and family were allowed to come with me to the doctor's office. I couldn't even sit still because I was so scared and shaky. After an interpreter had told me what to expect from an eye exam I calmed down. Then later when I had to go back again it was a lot easier.

I would like to go on now about the time I spent at the hospital after I had had my three children. It was a difficult time for me because my three children had died while I was at a hospital in Québec. When I was told that my three children had died, I really felt for my husband as I could not be with him. We had to go through so much without being able to comfort each other. I got really ill then after hearing about my children even though I had been cleared to go back home. My illness must have been pretty bad because they put me in intensive care. At that time, I did not care whether I lived or died. Later on I found out that I had come down with pneumonia. I was so sad not to be able to go home but when I finally did, I was happy. I survived the loss of my children with the support of my relatives. After I had been back for a while, I adopted a little boy, Arnaqo, whom I adore. When I got him I was so thankful that I could be blessed with another child.

What I enjoy very much is going fishing. Even late risers are anxious to go fishing. Listening to the wild birds while fishing is just beautiful. It's a wonderful feeling to start leaving camp to go fishing, and I think that all Inuit feel that way. After my husband died, I had thought that no one would be able to take me off fishing again, and I started to ignore my brothers. But it turned out that they were going to give me a lot of support. After I went through an operation, I didn't go fishing for a long time, but last year during the springtime I finally went again. It is wonderful to go off fishing.

I have always enjoyed making carvings, but now I just sit around because my hands aren't good any more for that kind of task. The only thing I do now is make drawings. It's as if my hands have gotten back at me. Although it is still very tiring, it's easier to make a drawing, so that is what I do now.

I will now continue in regards to my drawings. I enjoyed them all. After undergoing an operation on my hands, I have not carved into soap stone too much any more, but I've continued doing drawings on paper. It really scared me that I would not be able to draw any more after my operation but, with some encouragement, I have continued to be an artist. I have a lot more stories to tell even though I've written a lot already.

Owl
date unknown
white marble
41.7 x 44.5 x 26.3 cm
signed
Loaned by Samuel and
Esther Sarick
Art Gallery of Ontario,
Toronto, Ontario
S395

SUMMER OWL
1979
lithograph, 47/50
on wove, rag paper
printed by *Pitseolak
Niviaqsi*, 1947–
56.7 x 78.6 cm
Cape Dorset 1979, no.
L10 (uncatalogued)
Portfolio 1

*This is an owl which
has many flowers sur-
rounding it.*
1992 interview with Marion E.
Jackson and Odette Leroux

THE WORLD
AROUND ME
1980
lithograph, 7/50
on wove, rag paper
printed by *Pitseolak
Niviaqsi, 1947–*
56.6 x 79 cm
Gift of Theo
Waddington, 1982
Cape Dorset 1980, no.
6 (uncatalogued)
Portfolio II

I drew it just the way I usually draw. I really like those fish so I usually include them. I really enjoy fishing so I put them there even if I draw just as I'm imagining them…. This is an Inuit's hat. It's shaped like that, because back then, we used to have hats like those. They're anyone's faces.
1991 interview with Odette Leroux

They are birds' tails, but do not exactly look like real ones because they make the birds more attractive and those ones are part of the tail but behind them.
1992 interview with Marion E. Jackson and Odette Leroux

Not only that, I try to make them look the same. With those erasable pencils, I drew them correct by erasing until they look the same, which is at times, difficult. That's when I turn them out to look the same. By erasing and correcting, I make them look the

same. Through using an eraser, using a pencil, I shape them up the same, then with felt pen, I outline them when they look the same. That's the way I draw.
1991 interview with Odette Leroux

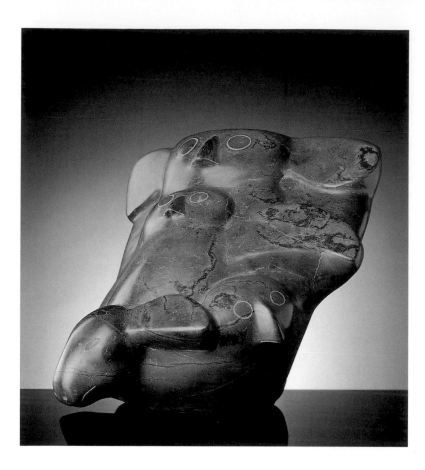

BIRDS
1969
dark green and black
stone
32 x 46 x 28 cm
unsigned
Loaned by Samuel and
Esther Sarick
Art Gallery of Ontario,
Toronto, Ontario
S895

*It looks like a drawing.
I try to make them
look, not like a pic-
turesque scenery, even
if it's a sculpture, I try
to make them look
more interesting out of
my imagination. This
one [at bottom] with
big ears, I think it was
supposed to look like a
dog. But it has big ears.*
1991 interview with
Odette Leroux

TWO OWLS
1977
light green stone
32.5 x 20 x 29.5 cm
unsigned
Canada Council Art
Bank, Ottawa
77-8-0592

OWL AND FRIENDS
1980
stonecut and stencil,
proof III (edition: 50)
on laid, kozo paper
printed by *Timothy
Ottochie, 1904–82*
49.5 x 60.5 cm
Cape Dorset 1980,
no. 13

*It is similar to the
other owl* (CD 1979,
no. L10, page 100,
SUMMER OWL), *with
the flowers and leaves
surrounding the birds.
I usually make them
resemble the others
because I don't like to
change too much with
any one of them.*
1992 interview with Marion E.
Jackson and Odette Leroux

*The way I do it is by
putting colour on the
paper. Anything or ani-
mals, I'll draw first,
then the landscape,
hills and the sky.*
1991 interview with Odette
Leroux

MOTHER NATURE
1980–82
green stone
36.5 x 36 x 31 cm
signed
Loaned by Samuel and
Esther Sarick
Art Gallery of Ontario,
Toronto, Ontario
S2256

*It's either a dog or a
polar bear. It's hard to
see it clearly. It's got it
in its mouth. Like
this...when female
dogs have to move
their pups around, they
have to carry them in
their mouths.*
1991 interview with Odette
Leroux

BIRD LANDSCAPE
1982
lithograph, 16/50
on wove paper
watermark: BFK
Rives/France
printed by *Pootoogook
Qiatsuq*, 1959–
51 x 66 cm
Cape Dorset 1982,
no. L9

This is also an ukpik.
*Also, this area has
some leaves. These are
twigs in the swamp
area and these don't
seem to have feet,
because they are down
in the water. The owl is
attacking the sand-
pipers in the swamp.*
1992 interview with Marion E.
Jackson and Odette Leroux

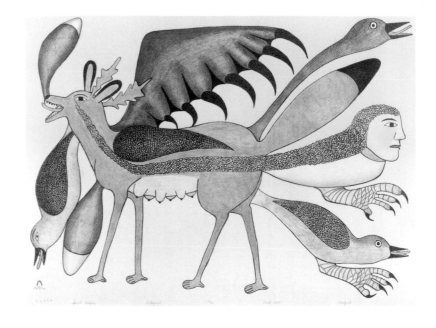

THE OWL BETWEEN
1982
lithograph, 17/50
on wove paper
printed by *Pitseolak
Niviaqsi*, 1947–
28.5 x 32 cm
Cape Dorset 1982,
no. L14

SPIRIT HELPERS
1989
lithograph, 47/50
on wove, rag paper
watermark:
Arches/France
printed by *Pitseolak
Niviaqsi*, 1947–
56.8 x 76.1 cm
Cape Dorset 1989, no. 8

*It is not exactly the
goddess, it is just from
my imagination…. I
never dreamed of any-
thing like that. It
seems like it, but I
never really like to
draw to make it real. I
can take a picture and
draw from it but I
don't. Animals also
have breasts, that's*

*why they are drawn
that way. I barely draw
any male figures. [I
draw women] because
I am a woman.*
1992 interview with Marion E.
Jackson and Odette Leroux

SPIRITS AT NIGHT
1989
lithograph, WBEC
proof I/V (edition: 50)
on wove, rag paper
watermark:
Arches/France
printed by *Aoudla
Pudlat, 1951–*
41.4 x 46 cm
Cape Dorset 1989, no. 9

*It doesn't make any
sense. But you can tell
that this is an image of
an animal, because
there are the tracks
here. This one with the
short tail and this one
is with the wings. It is
not exactly any type of
animal.*
1992 interview with Marion E.
Jackson and Odette Leroux

PROUD WOLF PACK
1990
lithograph, WBEC proof
II/III (edition: 50)
on wove, rag paper
watermark:
Arches/France
printed by *Pitseolak
Niviaqsi, 1947–*
57 x 76.5 cm
Cape Dorset 1990,
no. 3

*I drew these... as I was
dreaming. I had diffi-
culty drawing the foot-
prints.... Those are the
footprints, [they are]
supposed to be the
footprints anyway.
Some footprints
include prints of the
nails, like those of
dogs' footprints
imprinted on snow.
That's why their foot-
prints' nails look like
that....*

*I drew this on a flat
stone and not on paper.
I had difficulty draw-*

*ing some parts where
there is the white, the
grey and the black
ones. The drawing
chalks are too soft and
they get dark very easi-
ly. Some of these
[parts] are done with
harder drawing chalks
so they differ in tex-
ture. Some parts of the
drawing are done in
softer chalks and some
are done with harder
chalks.*

1991 interview with
Odette Leroux

NUNAVUT
QAJANARTUK
(OUR BEAUTIFUL
LAND)
1990
lithograph, hand-
coloured watercolour,
presentation proof (edi-
tion: 3)
on wove paper
watermark:
Arches/France

printed by *Aoudla
Pudlat, 1951–* and
*Niveaksie
Quvianaqtuliaq, 1970–*
76 x 116 cm
Gift of the Department
of Indian Affairs and
Northern Development,
1990
Cape Dorset 1990, no. 1
(uncatalogued)

I was asked if I could do a print about (our land) Nunavut for the land agreement that was signed in Igloolik. I started to do landscape drawings, I guess in 1986-1988, it was when I did those wolves (in lino block for Wolves in Spring *and the lithograph for* Proud Wolf Pack) *I started to do more drawings with mountains, rivers because I like them, and wanted to do more on the drawing.*

1 March, 1993. Information provided by Kenojuak Ashevak to Jimmy Manning upon Odette Leroux's request

NUNAVUT (OUR LAND) 1992
hand-coloured lithograph, proof (edition: 3)
on wove paper
watermark:
Arches/France
printed by *Pitseolak Niviaqsi, 1947–*
120 x 134 cm
Gift of the Department of Indian Affairs and Northern Development, 1994
Cape Dorset 1993, no. 1 (uncatalogued)

This is in every change of the season. Like the early spring, summer, fall where you can see newly formed ice and during the wintertime. During the time of longest daylight. This is all in the different seasons, like all year around.

This is the earth and the sky. This is the moon, and the moon starts to disappear, and this is the sun. This is the sky with everything in it, but this one is the moon and the stars. And the reason why the sun is in it as well, is that if these weren't here these couldn't have been here.

From here where the winter starts. This is the middle of winter.

That's why there's the dog team on the ice following the bear. This one is in the early spring, because it is still too early so part is the snow with the old tent on the top. This is still in the same season, so these are piled up waiting for the sun to be reflected as it is a drying rack. These are sleds and this is the place to put the sleds in the snow to protect the runners from the sun, because they are covered with the frozen mud. This is during the spring when it is time to be living in the tent, but there is still the ice. But the ice is starting to get some

holes, because it is springtime when a woman is fishing.

There are some small birds around. This is during the springtime when the ice is all gone. These two qajaak are following the white whales. These two people notice hunters following the whales, so they run. And in this one, autumn comes, and the ice is starting to form. Those are newly formed ice. This man went out hunting, and has one seal loaded in his qajaq. There is some snow in this area now. This is the lake flowing down to the sea water. And this is the sign of the freezing time in the lake.

The materials that we used consisted of four pieces to be put together. It was already a circle when I made it. I put four pieces together and I was very careful to make it exactly a circle. I used a pencil to make it even with a thin point and then with the wider utensil to make it a circle like this.

1992 interview with Marion E. Jackson and Odette Leroux

Syllabic inscriptions on
the lithograph (clock-
wise, starting at the
top): Longer days in the
year sliding with seal-
skins; Springtime;
Summertime; In the
fall during first snow-
fall; Middle of winter.

Qaunak Mikkigak

I like to carve human figures the most, especially those of women.
It's challenging to try and make their faces feminine-looking....
This is a seal-oil lamp and when our parents used to live in the igloos
it was very useful to make some water or cooking
as well as keeping the place warm.
Qulliit were valuable to the woman as they were the most important thing
for the whole family to have around.

1991 interview with Odette
Leroux and 1992 interview with
Marion E. Jackson and Odette
Leroux

Qaunak Mikkigak
1932–

One of the first women to begin carving and an artist steeped in the traditional Inuit culture, Qaunak Mikkigak has lived her entire life in the area around Cape Dorset. She was born in 1932 in the camp, Nuvujuak, and grew to maturity knowing the traditional Inuit camp life. After a temporary and unhappy adoption as a young child, Qaunak was reunited with her own family and lived in Cape Dorset and in various South Baffin camps including Nurata but, most frequently, stayed at Nuvujuak. As a youngster, Qaunak took pride in learning traditional women's ways and in helping her mother, Mary Kudjuakjuk, who suffered a heart condition and had difficulty moving about. Qaunak recalls that, when she was a young girl, a number of the men at Nuvujuak, including her father Pitseolak, carved small figures in ivory or stone to sell to the Hudson's Bay Company. She herself did some carvings at that time, though she was very shy about this because only the men were carving at the time. Qaunak's father died when she was still quite young, perhaps eight or ten years old. Her widowed mother re-married a

man named Quppapik and later moved with him to Churchill, Manitoba, for a period of time for Quppapik's employment.

Remaining behind in Nuvujuak, Qaunak married Oqutaq Mikkigak and continued in the traditional Inuit lifestyle. Later, when her parents returned from Churchill to Cape Dorset for Quppapik to become a custodian at the school, Qaunak and Oqutaq also moved into the settlement so that their two young children could attend the new school. At that time, James and Alma Houston were encouraging carving and sewing, and Qaunak responded enthusiastically to the opportunity to make things and to contribute to the support of her young family.

Qaunak and Oqutaq have raised eight children, seven of them adopted, and Qaunak has continued her active involvement in the arts. In the mid-1970s, she participated in the Cape Dorset jewellery project and has also done some drawing and sewing, but she remains best known for her strong naturalistic sculptures. Qaunak Mikkigak's images were included in the annual Cape Dorset print collections in 1980, 1981 and 1986, and her work has been included in several group shows including *Eskimo Sculpture, Eskimo Prints and Paintings of Norval Morrisseau*, Art Association of Newport, Rhode Island (1968); *Debut—Cape Dorset Jewellery*, Canadian Guild of Crafts

Quebec, Montréal (1976); *Things That Make Us Beautiful/ Nos Parures*, Department of Indian Affairs and Northern Development, Ottawa (1977-78); and *Northern Exposure: Inuit Images of Travel*, Burnaby Art Gallery, British Columbia (1986). Her art is included in a number of important public and private collections, including the Art Gallery of Ontario; the Canadian Museum of Civilization; the Inuit Cultural Institute, Rankin Inlet; the Laurentian University Museum and Arts Centre, Sudbury; the National Gallery of Canada; the Prince of Wales Northern Heritage Centre, Yellowknife; and the Winnipeg Art Gallery.

Also known for her ability for traditional Inuit throat singing, Qaunak has travelled widely in Canada and internationally to give throat-singing performances. Like her husband, she also holds regular employment as a custodian and takes pride in being able to provide well for her family.

facing overleaf:
THE REAL WOMAN
1990
dark green stone
44.5 x 23 x 17.5 cm
signed
IV-C-5499

Adopted Child

Qaunak Mikkigak

I WAS BORN in an igloo on 15 November, 1932, during the cold winter at Nuvujuaq. My mother, whose name was Kudjuakjuk, cooked and melted ice with only a stone lamp. When I grew big enough to help, I fetched ice and took out the *qurvik* to empty it because my mother had developed a heart problem. We enjoyed life in those days.

My first recollection is of the time my younger brother was being carried in an *amauti* and we were travelling to Cape Dorset by dog team. It is my first recollection of being afraid, when we came across another camp. We stopped there and three women came to greet us with a small sled. Without saying anything, one of the women put me on the sled to pull me to their camp. I was so afraid because a woman I didn't even know just put me on the sled. I remember I kept almost falling off, but there was someone to keep me on. The next thing I remember is sitting on the bed where there was an old woman who was going to be my adoptive mother, and I just kept crying. Someone thought maybe I was hungry and brought me some meat. I remember being told to eat the meat, but I forget what happened after that. It was almost like going to sleep until the next winter.

My next memory is when it was wintertime and my adoptive parents stopped loving me. Apparently, those parents used to treat children who weren't their own by beating them right from the start. I don't remember this, but apparently I was told to go outside. I remember being afraid of being beaten. I had four older brothers; the oldest of those was not shy of showing me love. Neither was this older brother's wife; she would make sure I had something to eat whenever we were alone. But none of the other brothers seemed to care.

I would keep company with Napachie Tukiqqi, who could not walk and whose father, Tukiqqi, acted as an Anglican preacher in the outpost camps. There would be times when I would keep Napachie company all day, and her family would feed me. We would play games, and Napachie taught me and my friend, Annie, the art of throat singing. Annie was also an adopted child like myself. I spent most of the winter there. During the spring my father, Pitseolak, came to visit at that camp which was called Kangisujuak. My father did not know that I was being mistreated, but he had started to miss me. Inuit didn't have radios then, so if they wanted to see someone they had to travel by dog team during the spring or by boat during the summer season. When my father was leaving, I stood by his *qamutik* because I did not want to be left behind. I remember that I was later returned to my mother in Cape Dorset during the spring season. I don't think my mother was serious that she wanted me back, but she started to cry when she removed my clothing because I had bruises and marks all over my body. I couldn't even dress or undress myself, maybe because I was too young or maybe because I was so badly mistreated. I couldn't feed myself either. I don't think I was any older than three or four at the time.

I have not told this story before, except to a few people, but I hope it will help people understand how much even little children know. The experience affected my life and has made me more understanding. I have one child of my own and seven adoptive children; I wanted to give them the love I didn't receive from my adopted parents.

In those days before wood was available, in the wintertime we lived only in igloos. They appeared to be quite large then, but I don't think they were. My father would make an igloo by compacting what little snow there was in the fall. It was so cold that my brother and I would be wrapped together to try and keep each other warm because the igloo was warmed only with a *qulliq*. It was so cold, especially if you had to use the *qurvik*. In those days, while my father was making an overnight shelter, we would stay wrapped up in skins to keep warm. My mother would start to warm up the igloo with only

a lamp and melt ice for drinking water because then we didn't have Coleman stoves. We used the blubber of the square flipper seal for oil for our *qulliq* and we would use moss to light it. I also remember my father making sure that he took moss along that had been soaked in seal oil whenever he went hunting. I remember that as the igloo got older, it got warmer because all the cracks got sealed in. Also, piling snow around the igloo made it better.

We would buy caribou skins and caribou sinew at the Hudson's Bay Company. When caribou were scarce because the migration path was too far away, we had to buy different kinds of skins and thread to sew clothing. My mother made all our clothing by chewing the skins to soften them up, drying them and softening them up some more. As we children got older, we were taught more about what women were supposed to do. We did all kinds of things, like helping to bring things into the igloo, fetching water and preparing seal blubber for lamp oil. We thought we were helping, but all the time we were learning.

In the fall—when we were still living in a *qarmaq*—before we moved into an igloo, I would go along with my mother when she went with a small sled to fetch willows for firewood. We would collect a whole bunch at a time and place them where there wouldn't be any snow so we could have enough for the following winter months. The piles would become so high they looked like big boulders. Then, during that winter, my mother and I would fetch some of the piled-up firewood as we needed it. Later my mother developed a heart condition, so I started fetching firewood on my own because she had taught me enough to do things on my own.

I learned a lot from doing things with my mother, but there were times when it was better to do things on my own— like taking the *qurvik* out to empty and cleaning the floor of the igloo—since I was the only help my mother had. Since it was necessary, I learned to do things.

I also remember my father making carvings out of ivory tusks for the Hudson's Bay Company, using a bow drill that had to be held on with his mouth. I also remember him going off for days to hunt and trap with my brother. My brother was very small then. My father died when I was quite young.

Later, after my father died, I started making soapstone heads for dolls, and later on I carved *qulliit*, then geese. I used to be so shy of the other women because they were not doing much carving then like the men did at the time. I still enjoy making carvings of Inuit and animals using an axe and file, but I have never used any electric tools. I had also started sewing with the encouragement of Saumik [James Houston] and Arnakutaaq [Alma Houston]. I started making carvings because I wanted my children to be able to afford things and so that I could help my husband financially.

Owl
1965
green stone
14.5 x 26 x 10.4 cm
signed
Gift of M.F. Feheley,
Toronto, Ontario, 1988
National Gallery of
Canada, Ottawa
No. 30077

I do my style totally on my own. I started on my own style when I started to carve.
1991 interview with Odette Leroux

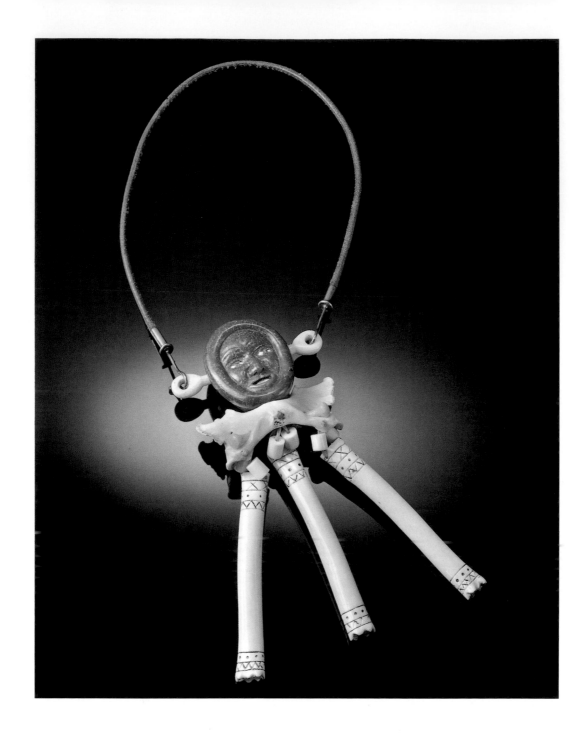

NECKLACE
1976
stone, ivory, bone,
sinew, leather and metal
36 x 7.8 x 3 cm
Gift of the Department
of Indian Affairs and
Northern Development,
1989
Inuit Cultural Institute,
Rankin Inlet,
Northwest Territories
2.77.15 ab

*I really like those too.
They are original and
are made out of bones
of seal and these are
geese bones. I made
sure that these parts
look like the ones I
used to have. I made
them look that way so
they don't just hang
from that piece. That
other one is made from*

*a seal's neck base—
vertebrae... (which is
underneath the face
and it is the last verte-
brae connecting to the
head of the seal)....
They are bones of goose
wings. I put them there
to ensure the necklace
looks and feels solid....
Ivory on the part of the
head.... They [the*

*bones of the goose] are
engraved... they are
just decorations...
[engraved with] electric
engraving tools....*
1991 interview with Odette
Leroux

BELT POUCH
1976
sealskin, red fox fur,
ivory, wool, sinew,
thread and cotton cloth
16 x 13.5 x 5 cm
Gift of the Department
of Indian Affairs and
Northern Development,
1989
Inuit Cultural Institute,
Rankin Inlet,
Northwest Territories
2.77.16

It's a small pouch where you carry your money. I made it while thinking about those some of us who tend to lose their money and I thought perhaps if we had our pouches there as necklaces, we would not lose our money so much.
1991 interview with Odette Leroux

NECKPOUCH
1976
ivory, claws, sealskin,
stone, thread and nylon
44 x 9.5 x 4 cm
Gift of the Department
of Indian Affairs and
Northern Development,
1989
Inuit Cultural Institute,
Rankin Inlet,
Northwest Territories
2.77.17

These are polar bear heads. They are where the necklace is supposed to be clipped together. I thought they would look better if I made them anything else but just plain-looking latches.... This is fur of seal. It is all sealskin.... A dark piece of soapstone. It is the feature of the necklace to make it look interesting.... and ivory.
1991 interview with Odette Leroux

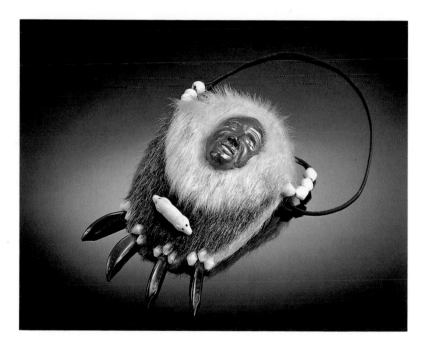

The jewellery on pages 118, 119 and 120 was submitted in 1976 for a competition/ exhibition entitled *The Things That Make Us Beautiful*. The *Neckpouch* on this page received an Award of Excellence for the use of indigenous material.

NECKPOUCH
1976
stone, ivory, sealskin, thread and nylon
43.5 x 16 x 4.5 cm
Gift of the Department of Indian Affairs and Northern Development, 1989
Inuit Cultural Institute, Rankin Inlet, Northwest Territories
2.77.23

I just used my imagination in making those but I made them so that they look more interesting.
1991 interview with Odette Leroux

NECKLACE
1976
ivory, stone, metal and sinew
30 x 11 x 2 cm
Gift of the Department of Indian Affairs and Northern Development, 1989
Inuit Cultural Institute, Rankin Inlet, Northwest Territories
2.77.24

All of those are ivory.... We used to have necklaces like those and I really used to admire them when I was a little girl. So I made them out to look like the ones I used to have.... I made them in contrast with each other because I liked it that way. They look long and thin, not thick, and I attempted to make them look interesting thin also.
1991 interview with Odette Leroux

Spring Geese   lithograph 24/50 Dorset 1980   Haunak

SPRING GEESE
1980
lithograph, 24/50
on wove, rag paper
printed by *Pitseolak
Niviaqsi, 1947–*
25.7 x 33 cm
Cape Dorset 1980,
no. L5

*Watching birds walking very fast in a way that they are just about to take off in flight, like we all do with interest. Those are... depicting birds just about to fly away, running very fast before taking off....
[The flowers]... I made those out of my imagination. I don't even know what kind they are supposed to be.*
1991 interview with Odette
Leroux

SHAMAN
circa 1977
green stone
41.9 x 12.8 x 7.6 cm
signed
Collection of the
West Baffin Eskimo
Co-operative, Cape
Dorset, Northwest
Territories
No. 1785

A shaman. The shaman usually turned to or used the animals as their spirits. This one is a seal. A man and his spirit.... I never saw one but I used to hear about them.... I did this because hardly anybody else portrays them, so I like doing different things.
1992 interview with Marion E. Jackson and Odette Leroux

FIRST GOOSE
OF THE SPRING
1981
stonecut and stencil,
49/50
on laid, kozo paper
printed by *Saggiaktok
Saggiaktok, 1932–*
63.5 x 63.2 cm
Cape Dorset 1981, no. 8

*You know, when geese
first arrive here in the
spring, they seemed to
be afraid of us when
they see us coming near
them. I made that in
that scene just because
I thought about them in
that state.*
1991 interview with Odette
Leroux

GEESE IN SPRING
1981
lithograph, 48/50
on wove, rag paper
printed by *Pitseolak
Niviaqsi, 1947–*
51.3 x 66 cm
Cape Dorset 1981,
no. L4

*I used to enjoy drawing
birds the most when I
drew every time and
thought that they were
the least difficult to
draw, so I tended to
draw them more.*
1991 interview with Odette
Leroux

REACHING FOR FISH
1987
green stone
24.8 x 12 x 44.5 cm
unsigned
IV-C-5491

He is holding a fish with his hands because when we are eating a fish we would hold it with the hands. The sea gulls really like to eat fish as well. So those are sea gulls going after fish…. Now, we rarely make any hands, as Inuit, but once I made a hand holding a fish. I made this from back then remembering that I liked making that carving. But I wasn't too sure what to make of this part through so I made it out to be a bird.

1992 interview with Marion E. Jackson and Odette Leroux and 1991 interview with Odette Leroux

**TERN SWOOPING
MAN AND WOMAN**
circa 1987
green stone
13.5 x 5 x 2.9 cm
18 x 5 x 4.7 cm
signed
IV-C-5481 ab

[The bird] sits there. The reason I put it there upside down was because it was thin, the head is that way because the bird is biting, and is coming from up there anyway, so it's shaped that way too.
1991 interview with Odette Leroux

A woman is in an amauti. The man is in traditional clothing. These are Arctic terns. When we were kids we used to be afraid of the terns when we were around terns' nests, because they go right

after you when you go near the nests. So, these figures are among the terns, and the terns are very protective of their eggs. So the couple is also protected, themselves, from the birds.
1992 interview with Marion E. Jackson and Odette Leroux

SHAMAN PERFORMING
circa 1988
green stone
56 x 13.5 x 13 cm
signed
IV-C-5480

I wanted to make it so that I do not waste any of the stone.... Some birds prefer fish and some of us prefer them too. So, as a result, I made it look like a bird going after it.... The man is kneeling. And this man is a shaman. These are his spirits that are invisible. This might be a bird. He is the only one who knows that they are such as his spirits. If I am the shaman, only I would know that they are not real animals. But the spirit turns to animals. Both the fish and the bird are supposedly invisible. Only this man knows that they are spirits. The shaman is performing his rites.

1991 interview with Odette Leroux and 1992 interview with Marion E. Jackson and Odette Leroux

SELFISH HUNTER
1988
green stone
47 x 33 x 8 cm
signed
Collection of the
Houston North Gallery,
Lunenburg, Nova Scotia

The Lake Trout.
I think it is a legend if it is not a true story. It's about this man, who made an igloo away from his wife, because he was a poor hunter. He left his wife behind and went to find this lake that had enough fish, but he was hiding it from his wife. Whenever he got back to his wife he would only bring back the smallest fish. He would travel all by himself. When he got home his wife usually noticed that he would be thirsty. Just as if he had something to make him very thirsty, but he would keep on drinking water regularly. Much later, his wife finally followed his tracks behind him and saw what he was up to. When the man reached his igloo the woman peeked inside the igloo after her husband entered it. Much to her surprise her husband was eating some fish. He had so many fish in his second place that he had been hiding from his wife, and they were huge fish. *While the woman was watching him eating a fish, suddenly the man choked and he was trying to get it out of his throat and making noises. While his wife was watching him choking she said to him, "Let the fish bone get stuck in your throat!" Sure enough he went out with a fish bone in his throat, walking around and around outside of his igloo before he died. After he died, then the woman examined the inside of the igloo and there were many large fish inside the igloo. It's when I was thinking about that story that I made this. It is a legend that I used to listen to while it was told. My mother used to tell it to us.*

1992 interview with Marion E. Jackson and Odette Leroux

SEDNA FRIGHTENED
BY WEIRD CREATURE
1988
green stone
29.4 x 9.2 x 61.2 cm
signed
IV-C-5482

*This is the sea goddess
covering its ears
because it is scared. I
have never seen this sea
monster....*
1992 interview with Marion E.
Jackson and Odette Leroux

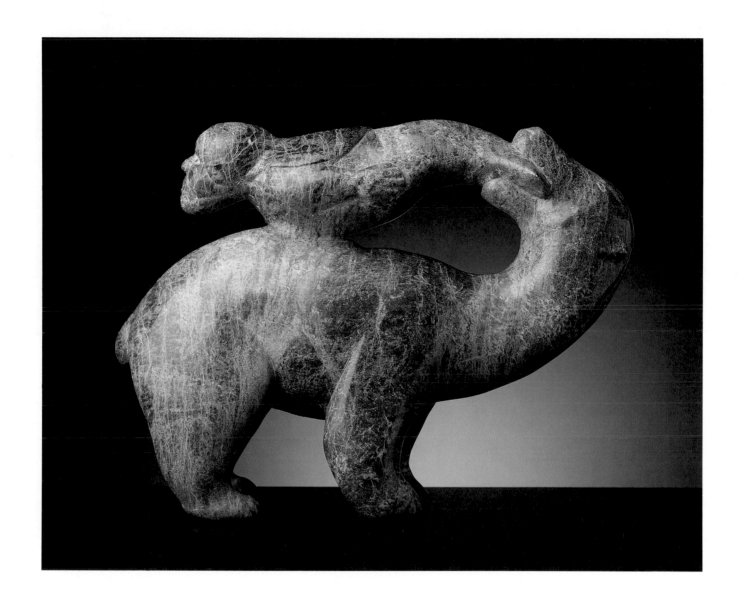

NANOOK
EATING SEDNA
1988
green stone
37.5 x 49 x 17.5 cm
signed
Collection of the
West Baffin Eskimo
Co-operative, Cape
Dorset, Northwest
Territories
4577 H

*The polar bears can eat
just about anything
that is alive.*
1992 interview with Marion E.
Jackson and Odette Leroux

HEAD WITH HANDS
AND WEBBED FEET
1991
green stone
11.6 x 18 x 4.3 cm
signed
IV-C-5484

*It was supposed to be a
man in the beginning...
and went through
transformation....
These are birds' feet. I
think these are human
hands. It was just from
my own imagination.*
Quotes from a meeting on 7
March, 1991, of the artist with
Minnie Aodla Freeman and
Odette Leroux and in a 1992
interview with Marion E.
Jackson and Odette Leroux

HEAD WITH HANDS
1991
green stone
9.5 X 20.3 X 3.2 cm
signed
IV-C-5502

Napachie Pootoogook

I was just a small child then,

    so I don't have any memory of seeing it damaged.

I heard people saying that the ship was cut in half—

    I vaguely remember seeing it with just the half showing—

I tried to depict that in my drawing.

1991 interview with
Odette Leroux

Napachie Pootoogook
1938–

One of six offspring of the highly acclaimed Cape Dorset artist, Pitseolak Ashoona, Napachie Pootoogook is a member of an extremely prolific artistic family. Like her mother, Napachie is well known for her graphic works, while four of her brothers—Qaqaq, Komwartok, Kiuggaq and Ottokie—have achieved a high level of recognition for their sculpture. In addition, Napachie's husband, Eegyvudluk Pootoogook, is a son of the famous South Baffin camp leader, Pootoogook, and was a long-time printmaker at the West Baffin Eskimo Co-op before failing eyesight led to his recent retirement .

Napachie lived on the land in the traditional lifestyle as a young child and through her teenage years, but has resided in Cape Dorset since the settlement first began to grow in the early 1960s. Napachie began to draw at about that time in response to James Houston's giving sheets of drawing paper to her mother and to her and inviting them to draw. Shy at first, Napachie appreciated the opportunity to earn some income through

drawing and found that she liked creating visual images and recounting traditional Inuit experiences through her images. While Napachie's drawing career has been interrupted from time to time as family and other necessities dictated, she has persisted in drawing for more than three decades. Her work has been included in fourteen Cape Dorset print collections since 1960, with forty-two prints issued in these collections.

Napachie's images have also been included in several important group shows of Inuit art including *Images of the Inuit from the Simon Fraser Collection*, Simon Fraser University, British Columbia (1979-81); *Eskimo Games: Graphics and Sculpture*, National Gallery of Modern Art, Rome, Italy (1981); *Arctic Vision: Art of the Canadian Inuit*, touring exhibition organized by the Department of Indian Affairs and Northern Development and Canadian Arctic Producers (1984-86); *Inuit Women and their Art: Graphics and Wallhangings*, University of Missouri (1988); *Night Spirits: Cape Dorset 1960-1965*, Winnipeg Art Gallery (1988-89); *Spoken in Stone: An Exhibition of Inuit Art*, Whyte Museum of the Canadian Rockies, Banff (1989); *Art Inuit, la*

Sculpture des Esquimaux du Canada, Thenon, France, and Liege, Belgium; (1989); and *Inuit Graphic Art from Indian and Northern Affairs, Canada*, Winnipeg Art Gallery (1989). In addition, works by Napachie Pootoogook are held by the Art Gallery of Greater Victoria; the Beaverbrook Art Gallery; the Canadian Museum of Civilization; the Glenbow Museum, Calgary; the Museum of Anthropology, University of British Columbia; the National Gallery of Canada; and the Royal Ontario Museum.

Napachie Pootoogook is the mother of ten children and is respected in her community for her understanding of the "old ways." She is an accomplished throat singer and has travelled in southern Canada and abroad with Qaunaq Mikkigak to demonstrate this traditional Inuit singing technique.

facing overleaf:
NASCOPIE REEF
1989
lithograph, 47/50
on wove, rag paper
watermark:

Arches/France
printed by *Aoudla Pudlat, 1951–*
44 x 48.9 cm
Cape Dorset 1989,
no. 18

My Mother's Teachings

Napachie Pootoogook

I WAS BORN in 1938. My first recollections are of the time we left our camp and went to Nettilling Lake, 100 kilometers north of Amajuak Lake, staying overnight at Ikirashaq before we started the long walk. As we left Ikirashaq, we all waved as we set off. I don't remember if it took us half a month or a whole month to get there, as I was only six or seven years of age. It was a tiring trip for my mother [Pitseolak Ashoona] because we young children did not make it easy for her. I remember that at that time our mother made all our clothing out of caribou skins. Life was good for us then because we were travelling with both our parents. But it turned out that my father died before we ever got there.

It was sad at times, too. I remember we grew up with the help of the other Inuit there who supplied us with food to eat. I am very grateful to the other Inuit who supported us. When we then moved to the coast, the Inuit there supported us too because my brothers—Namoonai, Qaqaq, Komwartok, Kiugaaq and Ottokie—were just young boys at the time. It is apparent now that my mother went through a rough time after my father died, especially having so many young children needing her care.

Even though it was very hard when we grew up, I am glad to be alive, glad that my mother brought me up. Now that I am older, I want to show appreciation, even for that rough time we had. I remember another time we moved; we didn't live at Cape Dorset then. Inuit did not stay in one place then; they travelled around with the help of dogs. We didn't even have dog-sleds then. I used to envy other girls who had fathers arriving home with food for them. We grew up only on what was given to us by other people. When my brothers were finally old enough to go hunting, it felt like we were very well off. Kiugaaq was the youngest of my three older brothers. But now he is getting pretty old because I am an old woman now, and I am younger than he is.

I want to thank the Inuit who help those in need with food, without charging for it. They do these things, but we have heard that is not the way it is in the South. The people in the South have a completely different way of life, and the population in their towns is very high. We have heard that there are some people in the South who help others in need as well.

The southern people in our community today are helping the Inuit by having them make carvings and drawings. The only difference seems to be that they pay money for the arts that are made. Even though I was brought up poor, I now have seven children who are living, but altogether I have had eleven children. Because of doctor's orders, I stopped having children even though I was still able. Today I have grandchildren whom I am very happy to have.

We lived at Iqaluit for two years, and I didn't like it there. It was too crowded, so I did not mind moving back here. Living in Iqaluit has its advantages, though. There is a hospital and staff there, and other things that are helpful to us as well.

When I was twenty-five years of age, I started doing drawings for Saumik [James Houston] along with other women. There were not that many people living at Cape Dorset then. Life was good then. I was a young woman with three children, and I was making drawings while my husband [Eegyvudluk Pootoogook] worked at the craft shop. It was fun when we got paid and we would go shopping. Then the prices were not so high. That was also the time we got our own house to live in, even though we had no heat or electricity.

It has not always been happy times between then and now. In 1963 or 1964, our house burned down, killing two of my children as well as one of my nieces. In those days we used a lantern for light, the kind that uses naphtha gas. Soon after that tragedy, another little girl, my five-year-old daughter, drowned. Even though I have gone through difficult times, I want to stay on my feet because there is nothing that can be done about it.

The Co-op has been very good for me by continuing to buy my drawings. I do not know the English language, but I have been making my living with drawings. The Co-op has always accepted my drawings, even though some are not so well drawn. That helps us very much financially as my husband has had to quit his job—because of his poor eyesight, not because he has gotten too old to work. My husband and I enjoy life, though we are aging now. Life is very different now, but that is okay because that is the way children are brought up these days. All Inuit children everywhere are now brought up to live differently, even my own children.

It is not any of my concern how other parents raise their children. I am just thankful that I was fortunate enough to have children because now they help me. I think it would be so lonely to live in a house all by myself. I am happy when they come to visit with me. I have done only a few carvings as I am not too good at that. I am not so young any more, so I have not done very many drawings lately. If I am asked to make something, I will try if I am able. I also enjoy hunting and fishing. I have enjoyed my life up to now and am happy when I remember back on it. I want to remember only the good times, not the bad that has affected my life.

Another experience I can remember that was not so happy was while my husband was off seal hunting. A polar bear came to our camp while my three children and I were alone. I was inside the tent, and my children were outside the tent playing while my husband went away for a few minutes to get a seal. My oldest daughter who was nine years old at the time had gone off to a hill to watch her father. All of a sudden, the other two children ran into the tent. My seven-year-old daughter was shouting, "There is a bear! There is a bear!"

We were so frightened because the polar bear kept trying to enter our tent. During the whole time my husband was away, the bear kept trying to enter the tent. Every time I half-turned away from the bear, it tried to get at my youngest child,

INUIT SEA DREAMS
1960
stonecut, Govt. proof
"B" (edition: 50)
on laid, kozo paper
printed by *Iyola
Kingwatsiak*, 1933–
49.5 x 60.8 cm
Cape Dorset 1960,
no. 42

The image is the whaling scene and telling a tale. Whales and bears and other animals turn into humans in Inuit mythology. It is depicting an Inuit myth even though I have not witnessed anything happening like that in real life.
1991 interview with
Odette Leroux

but I grabbed him to the safety of the tent. We were so afraid that I even poked at the bear with things in the tent to try to scare it away from us. Then I thought that if I poured gas on him, he would go away because he would not like the smell. As soon as it turned away because the smell of gas, we got out through the back of the tent and started running away from the bear. At this time I had a small rifle with me. One of my children started running towards where my husband was hunting.

All of these things I have experienced in my life are not all happy things. That's the way life is. My experiences in life include times that were frightening, times that were hard to deal with and happy times. I also tried different things—like drinking—things that were fun to do, things I did because I thought that was what I should do. Then, when I first started hearing about Jesus Christ, I found it very exciting, learning how I should lead my life; a good life, no sorrow, happy, no heavy burden to carry. I would also like other people to get to know Him as well.

I still lead my life that way, and people in the community have treated me well and still do. I also do drawings for the Co-op which I will continue to do for as long as I can. I have been drawing from the time I was very young, up to my middle-age years. But now my eyesight is not so good any more, like most elderly people. I enjoy my life as I get older. I have tried to live my life to the fullest. I will not try to become a "big person" just because of my experience in life. Because of the things I went through in life—both the bad and the good times—I have become a better person and I am grateful for that.

Even though I still have a lot I could talk about, I am having a hard time now thinking what to say. I would like to say that I have always really enjoyed going along on a fishing trip, but I have never really gone hunting because I am afraid to handle a rifle. I know how to sew with my hands or by using a machine, both traditional and modern clothing. I can use a skidoo but do not run a canoe because I am afraid to use the outboard motor. I am grateful for the chance to write about my life.

I would again like to mention just how dangerous the polar bears are, as are wolves. My three children and I were trapped in our tent by a polar bear while my husband was out seal hunting taking the rifle with him. I was so afraid when the bear tried to enter our tent, and we could not kill the bear because bears were being protected by the Greenpeace people who apparently do not know how dangerous they are. Bears can be very scary when they are bothering you because they are very large and powerful animals. My husband could not touch it because it's the law that bears be protected. I prevented it from entering our tent, and I don't want the polar bear population to grow too large. That's the story of my life.

BIRD SPIRITS
1960
stonecut, WBEC proof 4
(edition: 50)
on laid, kozo paper
printed by *Joanasie Salomonie, 1938–*
48.2 x 60.7 cm
Cape Dorset 1960,
no. 43

I have never seen a spirit. Perhaps if I saw a spirit, I would have a heart attack. I have heard people talking about having seen spirits. It would be quite a different story to me if I had seen one.
1979 interview with Marion E. Jackson

INUIT FAMILY
PLAYING BALL
1961
stonecut and stencil,
proof "A" (edition: 50)
on laid, kozo paper
printed by *Lukta
Qiatsuk, 1928–*
47.2 x 60.5 cm
Cape Dorset 1961,
no. 28

*They used to use ropes
in that sort of an activi-
ty. I have only heard
about it.*
1991 interview with Odette
Leroux

INUIT MOTHER
AND CHILDREN
FRIGHTENED BY
DEMONS
1961
stonecut, proof
(edition: 50)
on wove, kozo paper
printed by *Eegyvudluk
Pootoogook*, 1931–
51 x 76.5 cm
Cape Dorset 1961,
no. 78

UNTITLED
1962
engraving, proof (edi-
tion: 50)
on wove, rag paper
31.7 x 45.4 cm
Cape Dorset 1962,
no. 24

*I have not seen an
actual event happening
like that, but it used to
be done. [Inuit people]
used to have tents
made out of sealskins.
I made it because I
have heard about it
and here, that person is
hanging things to dry.*
1991 interview with Odette
Leroux

BIRDS FEEDING
1964
stonecut, proof IV
(edition: 50)
on wove, kozo paper
printed by *Lukta
Qiatsuk, 1928–*
42.3 x 51 cm
Cape Dorset 1964–65,
no. 78

BALL GAME
1966
stonecut, proof I
(edition: 50)
on laid, kozo paper
printed by *Lukta
Qiatsuk, 1928–*
62 x 85.9 cm
Cape Dorset 1967,
no. 21

*I created them to have
an image of people hav-
ing fun.*
1991 interview with Odette
Leroux

*I draw almost like my
mother's drawings.
Perhaps the reason why
is because I used to
watch my mother
drawing…. Even though
I don't try to copy what
she does, sometimes it
turns out that I draw
almost like my moth-
er's drawings.*
1979 interview with Marion E.
Jackson

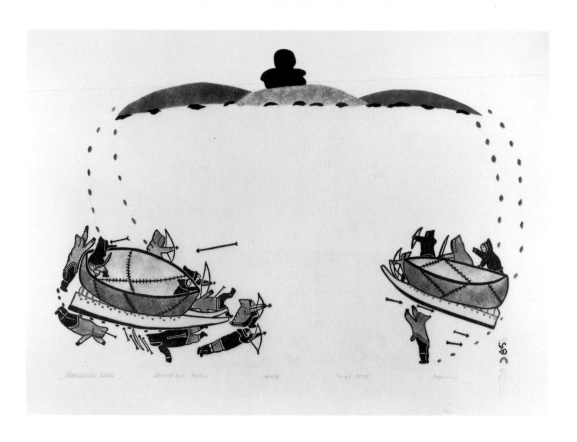

ATACHIEALUK'S
BATTLE
1978
stonecut and stencil,
proof (edition: 50)
on laid, kozo paper
printed by *Saggiaktok
Saggiaktok, 1932–*
56 x 71 cm
Cape Dorset 1978,
no. 53

*We used to know some
people who told these
stories. I used to listen
about such things from
the elders. It depicts a
true story.... I have to
enjoy what I draw. I get
very happy when I hear
comments about my
work. For example,
[this] story about
Atachiealuk, I enjoyed
it because it is an
unusual story. I like
doing things that have
a good and unusual
story.*
1991 interview with Odette
Leroux

*I have heard about a
man called Atachiealuk,
and of a battle between
people from northern
Quebec and people
from our side (from*
south Baffin Island).
*They hated each other,
and the Quebeckers
pretended that they
were after a boat even
though they really just
wanted to battle....*
1978 Cape Dorset Print
Catalogue, p. 61

*They battled using
bows and arrows
because there weren't
any rifles then.
Atachiealuk was origi-
nally from Sikusillaq,
and he and his wife
lived on one side of the
lake. As it turns out,
Atachiealuk was a
powerful man and was
unbeatable.... He was
able to catch the
arrows in midair, I sup-
pose he had divine
help.... He would view
the arrows like in slow
motion. He had a*
helper so they won the
*battle. Then they took
the women from the
other side when they
had won the battle.
And because the
women no longer had
husbands to help them,
he took over the job.
Atachiealuk was
unbeatable because he
was a smart man. I
drew this from what I
had heard of a true
story of Atachiealuk's
battle.*
Comment written by Napachie
Pootoogook in March 1991
about one of her favourite
prints.

WHALE HUNT
circa 1970
coloured pencil
on wove, bleached-
wood-pulp paper
49.7 x 61.3 cm
signed
Gift of Alma Houston,
Lunenburg, Nova
Scotia, 1979
IV-C-4801

The First Policeman 'I saw   Stonecut and Stencil   proof   Dorset 1978   Napachie

THE FIRST POLICEMAN
I SAW
1978
stonecut and stencil,
proof (edition: 50)
on laid, kozo paper
printed by *Laisa
Qajurajuk, 1935–*
62 x 72.5 cm
Cape Dorset 1978,
no. 54

*This scene depicts peo-
ple seeing them for the
first time with items
they want to trade.
These people are trying
to hide because they
are scared. It used to be
very scary to see a
policeman in the past.*
1991 interview with Odette
Leroux

FIRST SPRING TENT
1977
lithograph, 19/50
on wove, rag paper
printed by *Pitseolak
Niviaqsi*, 1947–
51.3 x 67.2 cm
Cape Dorset 1978,
no. L25

*They used to make
tents out of sealskins.
This depicts them
putting the tent up and
making the tent at the
same time.*
1991 interview with Odette
Leroux

SPRING DANCE
1979
stonecut and stencil,
proof (edition: 50)
on laid, kozo paper
printed by *Timothy
Ottochie*, 1904–82
51.3 x 71.5 cm
Cape Dorset 1979,
no. 36

*We had joy and fun just
like today. This depicts
people having fun and
they are dancing in
peaceful fun.*
1991 interview with Odette
Leroux

CARRIED OFF
BY A BIRD
1980
stonecut and stencil,
proof III (edition: 50)
on laid, kozo paper
printed by *Eegyvudluk
Pootoogook*, 1931–
52 x 60.5 cm
Cape Dorset 1980,
no. 28

*I made it out of my
imagination.*
1991 interview with Odette
Leroux

FLYING
NEAR THE RAINBOW
1980
stonecut and stencil,
proof III (edition: 50)
on laid, kozo paper
printed by *Timothy
Ottochie*, 1904–82
50 x 60.5 cm
Cape Dorset 1980,
no. 29

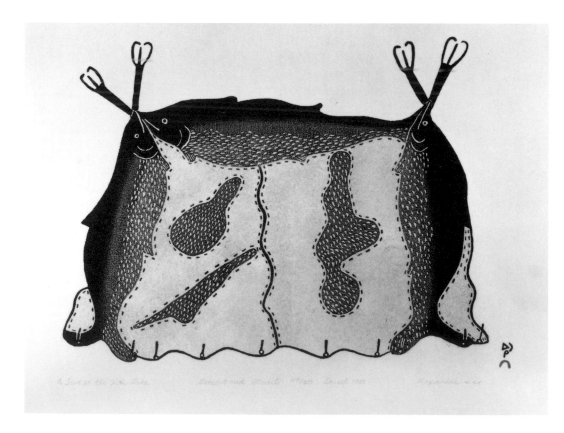

A TENT
AT THE FISH LAKE
1981
stonecut and stencil,
49/50
on laid, kozo paper
printed by *Timothy
Ottochie*, 1904–82
52.3 x 72.5 cm
Cape Dorset 1981,
no. 43

*I tried to put traditional
setting with decorations.*
1991 interview with
Odette Leroux

DRAWING OF MY
TENT 1982
stonecut and stencil,
43/50
on laid, kozo paper
printed by *Qabaroak
Qatsiya*, 1942–
63.5 x 86.7 cm
Cape Dorset 1982,
no. 36

*When I make my draw-
ings I try to make
[them] look good. This
scene depicts someone
doing some drawing
posing for someone to
take a picture.*
1991 interview with Odette
Leroux

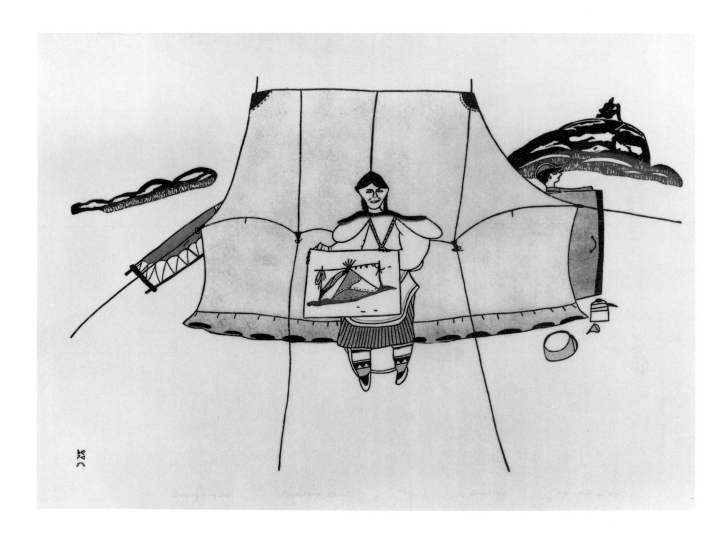

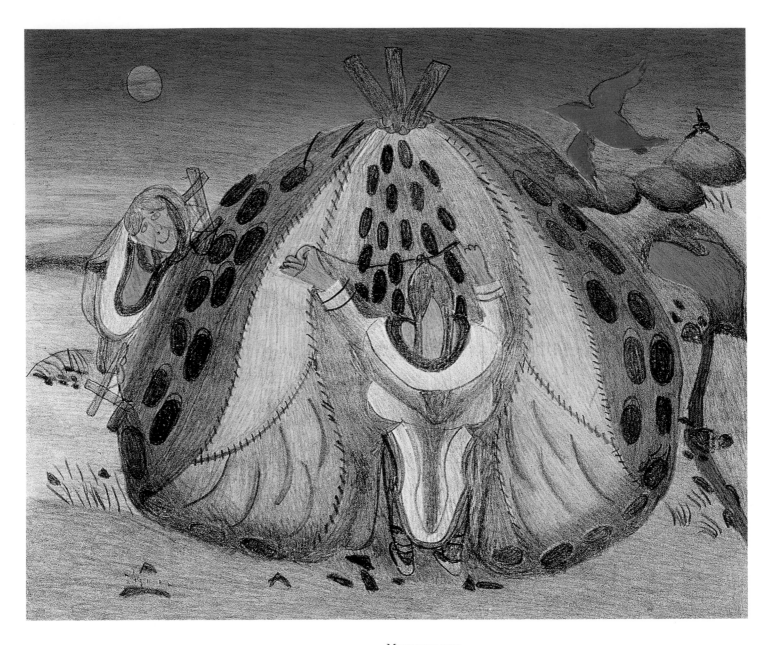

MENDING THE
SUMMER TENT
1989
lithograph, 47/50
on wove, rag paper
printed by *Pitseolak*
Niviaqsi, 1947–
46.2 x 51 cm
Cape Dorset 1989,
no. 20

MY NEW ACCORDION
1989
lithograph, WBEC proof
I/V (edition: 50)
on wove, rag paper
watermark:
Arches/France
printed by *Pitseolak*
Niviaqsi, 1947–
112.4 x 79.9 cm
Cape Dorset 1989,
no. 23

It was difficult to depict a person playing accordion.... I felt a great joy in completing it. It required my efforts most compared to all the other drawings I have made.
1991 interview with Odette Leroux

My drawing of accordion playing was a small drawing, so later on I found it too small and then I was trying to copy it to make it look bigger, but I had a hard time making the same one just with the pencil. That was when I was asked to make it look bigger, then I tried my best to draw it again just with the pencil first. Then when I had to do it on the lithograph, it was really hard work. My first drawing was much smaller than this one. It was very difficult... it is very hard even trying to make a copy of your own work.
1992 interview with Marion E. Jackson and Odette Leroux

SUMMER SCENE
1983
lithograph, 8/25
on wove, rag paper
watermark: BFK
Rives/France
printed by *Pitseolak*
Niviaqsi, 1947–
66.5 x 102 cm
Cape Dorset 1983,
no. L22

ROUGH ROUTE HOME
1990
stonecut and stencil,
WBEC proof II/V
(edition: 50)
on laid, kozo paper
printed by *Qiatsuq
Niviaqsi*, 1941–
57.7 x 71.7 cm
Cape Dorset 1990, no. 8

THE RIVER ROUTE
1989
lithograph, proof I/IV
(edition: 20)
on wove, rag paper
watermark:
Arches/France
printed by *Aoudla
Pudlat*, 1951–
43.2 x 48.4 cm
Cape Dorset 1989,
no. 19

*[While living] in
Nettilling [Lake, 100
kilometers north of
Amadjuak Lake] I used
to watch people carry-
ing heavy loads on
their backs and cross-
ing the river. So this is
from my memory. I
was thinking about
myself that time ago,
that's why I did that.*
1992 interview with Marion E.
Jackson and Odette Leroux

My Daughter's First Steps
1990
lithograph, WBEC proof
II/II (edition: 50)
on wove, rag paper
watermark:
Arches/France
printed by *Pitseolak
Niviaqsi, 1947–*
56.3 x 86.2 cm
Cape Dorset 1990, no. 9

I also made this one smaller and I had to make it larger than my original one. It's like this in my first drawing. We're usually holding the child like that. But I was told to do it this way when I did it in the stone. We used to go and wash our clothes right in the lake, so in this drawing there is the lake and the clothes are right around the lake. The woman is holding her child to teach it to walk. That is the way I did the drawing before I did it on stone. It was done differently in my original drawing. So it is quite different in the stone. Because in my original the woman is really caring for her child and loving her.
1992 interview with Marion E. Jackson and Odette Leroux

MAJUALAJUT
(UP THROUGH THE
ROUGH SHORE ICE)
1990
lithograph, proof II/V
(edition: 50)
on wove, rag paper
watermark:
Arches/France
printed by *Aoudla
Pudlat, 1951–*
76.3 x 56.8 cm
Cape Dorset 1990,
no. 10

*It is the name of the
hunter. It is a depiction
of them going through
pressurized ice. It used
to be that women used
to go and walk in front
to tantalize dogs to go
on.*
1991 interview with
Odette Leroux

WHALER'S EXCHANGE
1989
lithograph, 47/50
on wove, rag paper
watermark:
Arches/France
printed by *Arnaqo*
Ashevak, 1956–
40.6 x 50.9 cm
Cape Dorset 1989, no.
21

It is from my imagination. As for the historic scenes, I have not actually seen them. I used to know some half Inuit long time ago and I heard tales, that is why I have that style. I heard that the men used to trade their wives for some kinds of things—like tobacco or other things, with the white sailors. That is why there are half Inuit—it's because the sailors used to want women for an exchange of things even when or if a woman had a husband. I have depicted that scene from the things I heard about in the past, not because I have seen something like that happening.
1991 interview with Odette Leroux

This one [to the right] is a white man, and these are a couple—I depicted a white man asking to use the man's wife for a pot of tobacco in return. The Inuit men used to consent for their wives to be used by a white man.
1991 interview with Odette Leroux

WOMAN TODAY
1989
lithograph, WBEC proof
I/VII (edition: 50)
on wove, rag paper
watermark: BFK
Rives/France
printed by *Pitseolak
Niviaqsi, 1947*–
112.2 x 76 cm
Cape Dorset 1989,
no. 22

It is depicting the realities of life that I have experienced. It depicts real life as I know it today.
1991 interview with
Odette Leroux

Woman & Snow Bird   Proof II   Cape Dorset   1973   Pitaloosie

Pitaloosie Saila

I designed it like a shadow,

like one part of the face being in the dark.

As if it wasn't brightly lit in the home in those days.

Also, a face is different on both sides.

1992 interview with Marion E.
Jackson and Odette Leroux

Pitaloosie Saila
1942–

A graphic artist widely known for her 113 stunning images featured in twenty of the Cape Dorset print collections since 1968, Pitaloosie Saila comes from a family of extremely successful artists. Her husband Pauta is a highly respected sculptor, and her stepmother, Mary Pudlat, has been a regular contributor to Cape Dorset print collections. Pitaloosie's two uncles, Pudlo Pudlat and Osoochiak Pudlat, have both gained considerable attention for their graphic works, and her father's famous cousin, Peter Pitseolak, was one of the first South Baffin Inuit to produce a sustained body of artistic work over an extended period of years. However, Pitaloosie Saila began to draw completely on her own initiative in the early 1960s during the time that James Houston was at Cape Dorset, and her style is distinctively her own. She tends towards images of strong, nurturing women or women and children and frequently draws birds and mythical Taleelayu figures as well.

Perhaps more than any other artist in this exhibition, Pitaloosie Saila has had considerable experience outside the North. As a result of a spinal injury suffered in an accidental fall when she was seven or eight years old, Pitaloosie was hospitalized in southern Canada for seven years, not returning to Baffin Island until she was fifteen years old. In 1957, when she was healthy and able to return to her parents' camp at Keatuk, Pitaloosie spoke English and some French but had lost much of her native Inuktitut, and she found the re-adjustment difficult. Within a year, however, she married Pauta Saila and shortly thereafter began making occasional drawings for the new West Baffin Eskimo Co-op. Today, she has six surviving children and a number of grandchildren, and is recognized as one of the leading graphic artists in Cape Dorset.

Pitaloosie Saila has had numerous opportunities to travel in southern Canada and abroad in connection with her art. She spent the summer of 1967 in Toronto with their family while Pauta executed a carving for the International Sculpture Symposium. In 1974, Pitaloosie attended the opening of her first solo exhibition in Hamilton, Ontario, and subsequent showings of her work have taken her to major cities in southern Canada, the United States and Europe. In 1977, Pitaloosie's 1971 print, *Fisherman's Dream*, was featured on a twelve-cent Canadian postage stamp, and her 1980 print, *Arctic Madonna*, was selected for a UNICEF greeting card in 1983.

Graphics by Pitaloosie Saila have been included in a number of exhibitions of Canadian Inuit art that have toured internationally, including *The Inuit Print / L'estampe inuit*, organized by the Department of Indian Affairs and Northern Development and the National Museum of Man (now the Canadian Museum of Civilization) (1977-82); *Grasp Tight the Old Ways: Selections from the Klamer Family Collection of Inuit Art*, organized by the Art Gallery of Ontario (1983-85); *Arctic Vision: Art of the Canadian Inuit*, organized by the Department of Indian Affairs and Northern Development and Canadian Arctic Producers (1984-86); *Art Inuit, l'Art des Esquimaux du Canada*, St. Avold, France (1989-90); *In the Shadow of the Sun: Contemporary Indian and Inuit Art in Canada*, organized by the Canadian Museum of Civilization (1988-90); *Arctic Mirror*, organized by the Canadian Museum of Civilization (1990); and her graphics have been included in numerous exhibitions organized in major cities across Canada. Pitaloosie Saila's work is also represented in numerous private and public collections including those of the Art Gallery of Ontario; the Canadian Guild of Crafts Quebec; the Canadian Museum of Civilization; the Glenbow Museum, Calgary; the London Regional Art Gallery; the Macdonald Stewart Art Centre, Guelph; McMaster University Art Gallery; the McMichael Canadian Art Collection, Kleinburg; the Mendel Art Gallery, Saskatoon; the Montréal Museum of Fine Arts; the National Gallery of Canada; the Nickle Arts Museum, University of Calgary; the Simon Fraser Gallery, Simon Fraser University; and the Winnipeg Art Gallery. She continues to be a very prolific graphic artist and sees her art as a way to preserve the experiences and values of the Inuit culture.

facing overleaf:
WOMAN
AND SNOW BIRD
1973
stonecut and stencil,
proof II
(edition: 50)

on laid, kozo paper
printed by
Lukta Qiatsuk,
1928–
61.5 x 43 cm
Cape Dorset 1973,
no. 50

What I Remember

Pitaloosie Saila

I WAS BORN here in Cape Dorset in the early summer on 11 July, 1942. I was the first child in my family. There are great stories about my birth. My mother was in very hard labour. It took her three and a half days of hard labour. When I was born, there was great joy for my parents and their relatives.

Two and a half years later my mother died. I had a younger sister at that time, and she was just a baby. While my father was away on a walrus hunt, my mother died. At that time both of my grandmothers took care of me. My father's mother, Quppa, was like a mother and a grandmother at the same time. My sister was adopted to one of my uncles and his wife. That's the way I was told, and I don't remember anything about my mother.

Because I remember crying for something, it seems I remember only sorrow from the beginning of my life. The way I see it now, I think it must have been hard for my father when he came back from hunting and was told that his wife had died. My mother wasn't sick when my father left for the walrus hunt. He was gone for almost a month. He came back not knowing that his wife had died of sickness. I think she died a week after he left; it was the beginning of winter in the late fall. The way I see it now, they were a very young couple. That's the story of my mother and father and of myself.

One evening after my mother had been dead for about two years, just as it was getting dark, I remember being so happy when my father came back to our camp with my uncle (my mother's brother) and my cousin (son of my mother's deceased brother). Both my uncle and cousin have since passed away. That evening my father arrived with them by dog team, bringing a woman with them. We ran out to meet them when they arrived. When I saw a woman was with them, I ran back to my grandmother's and shouted that my mother had arrived with them. I was so happy. When I went back out to where they were, I stood by my father and asked him if my mother had come back. He did not reply for a few minutes. Then he said that she wasn't my mother but my aunt, a cousin of my mother. When he said that, I started crying because I understood then that the woman who had arrived with them was not my mother.

I walked back home and sat beside my grandmother and cried, facing the doorway and waiting for the woman to come in. As she came in, she stood by the doorway, and I just stared at her. She too just looked at us from where she stood. She looked and dressed so differently from us. She was wearing caribou clothing. Her *amauti* hood was a completely different style from ours. In those days, women always wore *amautiit* as this showed femininity. That was how it used to be. It turned out that this woman, who was to be my stepmother, and my mother were related; their grandfathers were brothers. My stepmother, Mary Pudlat, whom I call "aunt," was originally from Northern Quebec. She is also an artist.

I remember, too, as children we would play outside. One time during winter—though I don't remember exactly what month—three of us girls were pretending to be going for a walk up a hill to pick berries. It was a very nice day outside, I remember. We walked up the hill following old footprints, one by one. I was the last one as I followed them up the hill. The girl who was ahead of me kept sliding back so she started holding on to the one next to her. And she too kept slipping, so they both started sliding back. The girl in front of me held on to me and tried not to slip back as I was doing. Then she was pushed so she slid toward me. Then the one who didn't have anyone else to hang on to slid down. The one who had hold of my parka started sliding down so she grabbed my foot. Then we both were sliding down the hill. Then, as I watched her, she fell down the hill at great speed. She landed with a big thud at the bottom of the hill and started crying. The other girl slid down too, but I wasn't as aware of her. I broke my upper back from

that fall and was unconscious before getting to where I ended up.

From that fall down the hill, I had broken my upper back and was unconscious for a while. That is what I have been told by the woman who watched my fall. She has since passed away. She was out getting ice from the lake at the bottom of the hill when she saw me falling. She was living on the other side of the lake from where we lived. She had watched us girls as we tried to make it up the large hill, then witnessed our fall down the hill. Then she started running towards us, screaming with all her might. When she reached me, she didn't know whether I was dead or alive. As she had just witnessed my fall, she panicked when she reached me. She started calling for help as she carried me. She was met by my aunt, wife of my father's older brother. My aunt took me to my grandmother's as that igloo was the closest one. Because the men had gone hunting, my relatives—all women and children along with the other people from across the lake—gathered at my grandmother's igloo thinking that I had died. I was unconscious at the time. I had literally been dead for a few minutes. That was a very difficult time not only for me but for everyone there at that time.

Then the RCMP [officer] and his wife, who was a nurse, came to our camp from Lake Harbour. My father had asked them to come when they were passing through our camp on the way to Cape Dorset, so they came by dog team with my father. I remember being so afraid when they walked in. My father told me the nurse would examine me to find out what was wrong, assuring me that it wouldn't hurt. I was asked to take off my parka, but I refused. Someone that I didn't know took my parka off. I remember the nurse examined me, and her hands were so cold as she had just come from a long trip. My father apparently knew some English and they were talking. And as the nurse talked to him, he kept saying "yes" and "okay," so I got really angry with him that he was agreeing. I then understood that I would have to go away from home to

Lake Harbour by dog team, though I did not know when it would be. New clothing was made for me by the women in the way that my grandmother advised them.

My father, myself, and the policeman and his wife left by dog team for Lake Harbour, bringing along another young woman who is now a sculptor, Qaunak Mikkigak, and a man who had to go too because of some illness. The man was the husband of my late aunt, Kingmeata Etidlooie; she also became a graphic artist. I will always remember the time we left our camp, with relatives bidding us goodbye as the dog teams left.

On the way, we camped at another place overnight, and I recognized some people I knew. As we left the next morning, another patient came along, a young man who turned out to be my husband's nephew, Josephee. I remember he was crying, too, as we left. He has since passed away. I remember him well as he was my aunt's husband, and he was a kind man. I remember him telling the Inuit and *qallunaat* there that he did not want to leave, and when we were riding the sled, he used to jump off. Then when we stopped to have tea or something, I remember them trying to tie him down to the sled and I was feeling so sorry for him and not understanding why. They were only trying to help him. That is what I remember about Aguk being treated this way on our trip. Because my father was interpreting, I know he had said that he did not want to be sent away; and later I heard my aunt's husband committed suicide.

We came across maybe two more camps before arriving at Lake Harbour. When we arrived, the policeman and the other Inuit rested. So did my father for two or three days in order to be able to head back to our camp. My father and I stayed at an RCMP helper's place. Then one morning I woke up and could not find my father, so I started crying. I was then told my father had left and was told not to cry. I felt like I had lost my whole life. But out of love for me, my father left while I was still asleep.

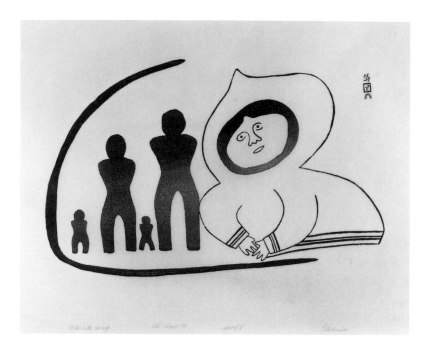

MY DOLLS
1967
(Original title: *Child with Carvings.* Changed by artist.)
stonecut, proof II
(edition: 50)
on laid, kozo paper
printed by *Lukta Qiatsuk, 1928–*
61.7 x 70.7 cm
Cape Dorset 1968,
no. 18

I drew this as it being myself, thinking of how I used to be then, the way I was dressed with a parka and my clothing. The way I remember how our dolls were clothed. Because I used to admire them.... That's what they were: the father, the mother and their kids.... I should have made another little girl to go with that one. But I was just thinking of myself perhaps.
1991 interview with Odette Leroux

These are traditional dolls that we grew up knowing. Inuit dolls that we played with, these were smaller sizes.... We used to dress them up.... They were the only precious toys I had. I didn't have any toys except for those. Dolls used to have a lot of matching sets to go with them. Some people used to have a lot of things to go with dolls. Blankets, sleds, anything, kamiik, amauti-it, all Inuit clothing and such.... We always sewed something to put on them. Any material to put on them.... That was the way young girls were taught what clothing was worn and how to make clothing.... There were kids that would come over to play with us. And they would bring their own dolls and stuff.
1991 interview with Odette Leroux

We then left for Iqaluit from Lake Harbour by dog team—the policeman, his wife, and some Inuit. As we were arriving at Iqaluit, I remember clearly the airplane would dive down then up again just over us. I remember another incident when the young woman, Qaunak Mikkigak, fell off the sled accidentally and was grabbed by the dogs from behind us. I thought she had been mauled to death, but she survived it by keeping her head protected.

While we were staying a few days in Iqaluit, I found that we had relatives there. Then we left for Halifax on a plane which was filled with patients. I was later told that someone had to carry me on their knees. I kept sliding down and the person got pretty tired out from having to carry me. It must have taken us a long time to get to our destination because in those days it took planes longer to get to where they were going. When we finally landed at Goose Bay (Labrador), I remember all the lights and cars coming to meet us. When we got to the hangar, we were served sandwiches but I wasn't used to the taste. We were then flown to Halifax where the hospital was. It was there that I first tasted ice cream. I remember the *qallunaat* who took patients out on passes trying to decide what food to buy, like sodas and ice cream that the Inuit could eat. Using sign language, one of the *qallunaat* appeared to have said that they would buy something like eggs. The Inuit too had trouble understanding. What they came back with was something else altogether!

There were quite a number of Inuit from different regions of the North, along with military patients at the military hospital in Halifax. I remember the commander of the soldiers came to visit the military patients bringing others with him. They entered our rooms as well. I must have looked quite frightened of them because I remember being told by Qaunak and another person not to be afraid. I was given some candy, and my photo was taken with the one who obviously was one of the military bosses. Today I still have the picture that was taken because someone else recognized my picture at the Hamilton hospital to which I was later transferred.

Another memory I have is when a woman came accompanied by a large group of people. I wonder even now if maybe it was the Queen, because I still see her on television. At that time the Inuit and *qallunaat* patients were taken outside to watch her; and then later we were taken to a stadium of some sort.

It was a long time ago—from 1950 to 1957—that I was in the hospital, and that's all I can remember. I doubt that the huge hospitals there have Inuit patients now. So many Inuit then were taken there to be treated, and some died there. Another hospital I was taken to is one in Montréal which even now receives Inuit patients.

I was also in another hospital; I am not sure exactly where it is, but I do know it is in Quebec. I remember while I was there, the nuns wore black with white hats to go with the uniforms. I don't know if the patients are still there. I did not enjoy my stay at that hospital at all because I remember being afraid of those nurses. They did not treat the Inuit patients very well then. I never once saw another Inuk patient there; it was like I was imprisoned there. I don't think the nurses knew how to be nice to patients. I remember one nurse especially because she didn't treat me very well at all. They were not all like that. At that time I did not understand English either, so I couldn't ask if there were other Inuit there. That nurse who mistreated me came in my room again and scolded at me to eat, but I couldn't because I was too sick and not able to feed myself. Sometimes I wonder if she might still be alive. I used to be so afraid of her because I could hear her when she was coming from the rustle of her clothing.

It was only once in a long while that I would be taken outside of the hospital, and that was the only time I saw other Inuit. It was also there in Montréal that I learned to speak

French because the people there spoke mainly French. I forgot my own language. When I did see other Inuit from different regions, I couldn't understand them because of their dialects. I spoke very little Inuktitut, but it became useful when I could interpret for some people. Those are my experiences, my memories of my stay there, what I saw, cried about, got hurt by, and got angry about. That's all I've got in me.

Some thoughts about my drawings: if someone likes the drawings that I make, it always encourages me to continue. Even if I myself do not like them and am not proud of them, it encourages me and I become proud of them and become proud of myself. There are quite a number of drawings I have made that have not been made into prints and are not on display. I am saying this, not because I liked those ones, but because I know how many drawings I have made. I draw what I have seen, what I have heard about, and what I remember. It is very difficult to know exactly what to draw as the piece of paper is completely blank, and you have to first create the drawing in your mind before it starts to come into being.

I started making drawings on my own, mainly because I wanted to but also because I wanted to start making an income. Now I can buy some of the things I want with the money I made from my drawings. I try to sit down every day to do my drawings as long as I am well. Perhaps my first drawing wasn't any good. I don't even remember what I first drew, but I do remember taking it to the craft shop. I envy the women who are quite talented to make things they want because, even now, I am not a great artist.

I found it very difficult when I first started drawing, and the money I made then was very small. Although I still have a hard time, I still make drawings. I still make a living by making drawings. The drawings I do are my heritage to my children, my grandchildren and future generations. I draw what I have seen or heard; I draw about my life. I draw so the Inuit traditional way of life can be preserved on paper, and it is only when I draw that it will be shown. We all make things based on our abilities. That is how it will always be.

Young Girl & Birds   Print 170   Proof III   Pitaloosie

YOUNG GIRL
AND BIRDS
1970
stonecut, proof III
(edition: 50)
on laid, kozo paper
printed by *Timothy
Ottochie*, 1904–82
42.7 x 60.8 cm
Cape Dorset 1970,
no. 15

*I drew that one out of
my own imagina-
tion.... Young people
used to have hair
braided like that....
Those birds came out
very well with those
hands shaped that
way.*
1991 interview with Odette
Leroux and 1992 interview
with Marion E. Jackson and
Odette Leroux

Flower Woman   proof III   Dorset 1970   Pitaloosie

WOMAN
1970
(Original title: *Flower Woman*. Changed by artist.)
stonecut, proof III
(edition: 50)
on laid, kozo paper
printed by *Eegyvudluk Pootoogook*, 1931–
37 x 60.8 cm
Cape Dorset 1971, no. 25

True Inuit women tend to have interesting facial features. Some of them must have been very attractive looking. I made that when I was thinking that and at the same time, thinking of their clothing. Like, caribous have antlers, that's what I was only thinking of when I drew it. I imagined their shoulders, and the hoods of their amautiit....
There is something about the flower in this, but I was thinking about the sealskin carrying parka with designs.

1991 interview with Odette Leroux and 1992 interview with Marion E. Jackson and Odette Leroux

FAMILY OF TWINS
1971
stonecut, proof III
(edition: 50)
on laid, kozo paper
printed by *Timothy
Ottochie, 1904–82*
44.2 x 62.3 cm
Cape Dorset 1971,
no. 32

My mother had older sisters who were twins. I myself had a twin. I was born with it but it was stillborn. A twin sister, but she wasn't formed normally. That's why my mother had a hard time delivering us. I also had an aunt who had twins. Three times. My grandmother had twins (my mother's mother), one of her twins had two sets of twins and another aunt had twins.... Sometimes they're boy and girl or two girls.... But they've never carried twins before in the amauti. *But one of them maybe would be here inside the* amauti.

1991 interview with Odette Leroux

INUIT LEADER
1972
stonecut, 37/50
on laid, kozo paper
printed by *Lukta Qiatsuk*, 1928–
70.1 x 85.5 cm
Gift of the Department
of Indian Affairs and
Northern Development,
1989
Cape Dorset 1972,
no. 11

I don't know Picasso, myself.
1991 interview with Odette Leroux

This is supposed to be a woman, with the woman's kamiik and baby packing parka.... Her amauti's hood is shaped that way. I imagined her to be a woman when I drew it. I've heard that back then, women used to have tattoos that meant they were "real women".... They were very serious about those tattoos back then. And back then, whether they were married or not, some women were
thought of as leaders by men.... I even found out that my father's mother, though she didn't have a husband, she had sons only, she was still the leader, only she didn't have any tattoos.... Yes, they had the power then. If their children stayed with them. And also when they had been married to the leader of the camp. Like, my grandfather.*
1992 interview with Marion E. Jackson and Odette Leroux and 1991 interview with Odette Leroux

In those days, women with tattoos were considered important. When people praised them after they did things that were important for people, then they would be tattooed. I don't know, I have never been told exactly for what. Only that it was done when that woman has done something that was unforgettable. My father used to tell me a story about a woman leader in one of those camps. That woman had skills some women didn't have. She helped some
people who had been shipwrecked and she took them to an island and they survived with her help. Everything was gone from the boat. That woman had a lot of knowledge, so they usually asked her for advice. She was a powerful woman; she was not bossy but she survived and saved the others. It's not only men are powerful, there are also some powerful women.*
1992 interview with Marion E. Jackson and Odette Leroux

ARCTIC MADONNA
1980
stonecut and stencil,
proof III (edition: 50)
on laid, kozo paper
printed by *Simigak
Simeonie, 1939–*
60 x 71 cm
Cape Dorset 1980,
no. 32

BIRD IN
MORNING MIST
1984
lithograph, proof
(edition: 50)
on wove, rag paper
printed by *Pootoogook
Qiatsuq, 1959–*
50 x 67.3 cm
Cape Dorset 1984,
no. 25

*This is another example
of my style of drawing.
Some I make by first
thinking about what I
would like to draw and
other times it just comes
to my mind. There are
times I cannot put on
paper what my mind
has created…. Again, I
have been told that a
lot of people like it….
The drawings that I
make, if someone likes
them, that always
encourages me to con-
tinue.*

Comment written by Pitaloosie
Saila in March 1991 about one
of her favourite prints.

SEA BIRD
1984
(Original title: *Bird Spirit at Sea*. Changed by artist.)
stonecut, proof
(edition: 50)
on wove, kozo paper
printed by *Eegyvudluk Pootoogook*, 1931–
64.8 x 98 cm
Cape Dorset 1984, no.26

I also did that one just the same as the earlier one. Only I thought of birds attempting to feed themselves by the shore. That was my image of birds feeding.... It's not starving, it's just trying to eat. Sea birds are all like that, they tend to eat out of the sea.... I don't know any spirit birds.
1991 interview with Odette Leroux

COURTING OWL
1985
stonecut and stencil,
49/50
on laid, kozo paper
printed by *Iyola
Kingwatsiak*, 1933–
63.6 x 77.9 cm
Cape Dorset 1985,
no. 20

*I never thought of it
that way.* Ukpik *with a
tail. I didn't like the
tail it came out that
way. . .. My hand was
just leading.*
1992 interview with Marion E.
Jackson and Odette Leroux

MOTHER'S WARMTH
1984
lithograph, proof
(edition: 50)
on wove, rag paper
watermark:
Arches/France
printed by *Pootoogook
Qiatsuq*, 1959–
50.3 x 67.4 cm
Cape Dorset 1984,
no. 29

*This one [is] kind of
large. I thought if I
made it large, it would
look interesting.
Making them large and
looking like owls. They
are mother and baby
birds. I like to do
drawings.*
1991 interview with Odette
Leroux

WOMAN OF OLD
1984
lithograph, proof
(edition: 50)
on wove, rag paper
printed by *Pitseolak
Niviaqsi, 1947–*
67.3 x 50 cm
Cape Dorset 1984,
no. 36

I drew that as a woman wearing an amauti *anyway, even though she doesn't have a baby in the pouch. Some women wear* amautiit *although they're not carrying a baby. Some older women too…. [I draw] what I want to draw and what I find I enjoy drawing when I really feel like drawing. I drew this one while I wasn't too sure how to draw. It was when I was still new at drawing that I did this one. I'm beginning to draw what I remember most and they're looking different from what I used to draw. What you're used to seeing before, I draw differently now than those drawings from that time.*
1991 interview with Odette Leroux

AFFECTIONATE
MOTHER
1985
stonecut and stencil,
49/50
on laid, kozo paper
printed by *Pee Mikkigak, 1940–*
79.2 x 56 cm
Cape Dorset 1985,
no. 18

SEDNA WITH FISH
1985
stonecut and stencil,
49/50
on laid, kozo paper
printed by *Iyola
Kingwatsiak*, 1933–
56.5 x 63.6 cm
Cape Dorset 1985,
no. 24

I've heard of a mermaid before, so I drew this out of that. Just by imagining one, because I wasn't sure what they look like. It turned out that way as I imagined it to look like. As it is, it has a legend behind it (Sedna).... Even now, people think that they *have seen her. There is no story of her, there just is some belief that there is one out there.*
1991 interview with Odette Leroux

NESTLING
1985
stonecut, 49/50
on wove, kozo paper
printed by *Saggiaktok
Saggiaktok*, 1932–
47 x 63.5 cm
Cape Dorset 1985,
no. 22

*I also enjoy drawing
birds. You know, when
birds have nests they
tend to always have
their heads bent down
with their wings almost
behind their bodies....
The way that they posi-
tion their legs even,
they tend to have an
odd position when
they're just aflight over
their eggs.*
1991 interview with Odette
Leroux

OOKPAGAQ
(YOUNG OWL)
1985
stonecut and stencil,
49/50
on laid, kozo paper
printed by *Iyola
Kingwatsiak*, 1933–
63.6 x 76.5 cm
Cape Dorset 1985,
no. 23

MOTHER
1981
lithograph, 48/50
on wove, rag paper
watermark: BFK
Rives/France
printed by *Pitseolak
Niviaqsi*, 1947–
66.6 x 51 cm
Cape Dorset 1981,
no. L25

*I had a mother, but she
passed away.... I just
don't remember her.*

*I tend to pay attention
to women, perhaps
because I don't have a
mother. Probably think-
ing that some women
are so powerful.*

*When we would visit
other Inuit's homes, the
way we used to, there
would be some women
who would seem larger
just because we were
smaller. I made that
thinking of those times.
Only I made this head
too small. Some of
those women would
look huge compared to
us, because we were so
tiny.*
1991 interview with
Odette Leroux

NESTLED OWLS
1986
lithograph, 46/50
on wove, rag paper
printed by *Pitseolak
Niviaqsi, 1947–*
51.4 x 71.6 cm
Cape Dorset 1986,
no. 24

*[Owls] tend to nestle
together, so those two
are behind her as a
result. The mother is
protecting her babies.*
1991 interview with Odette
Leroux

YOUNG MOTHER
AND CHILDREN
1985
stoncut and stencil,
49/50 on laid, kozo paper
printed by *Saggiaktok*
Saggiaktok, 1932–
63.6 x 46.8 cm
Cape Dorset 1985,
no. 26

OUT OF THE SEA
1986
stonecut and stencil,
44/50
on wove, kozo paper
printed by *Saggiaktok
Saggiaktok*, 1932–
55.5 x 71.2 cm
Cape Dorset 1986,
no. 25

*I made that one with
an* ulu *because she's a
female even though she
is a mermaid.*
1991 interview with Odette
Leroux

MOULTING OWL
1985
lithograph, 49/50
on wove, kozo paper
printed by *Aoudla
Pudlat, 1951–*
56.5 x 73.3 cm
Cape Dorset 1985,
no. 27

*I just drew that one as
well. People can have
different views of owls.
That's what I thought
when I drew it. Even as
Inuit here, we tend to
get surprised and excit-
ed when we see an owl.
We say, "Hey, look at
that owl!"*
1991 interview with Odette
Leroux

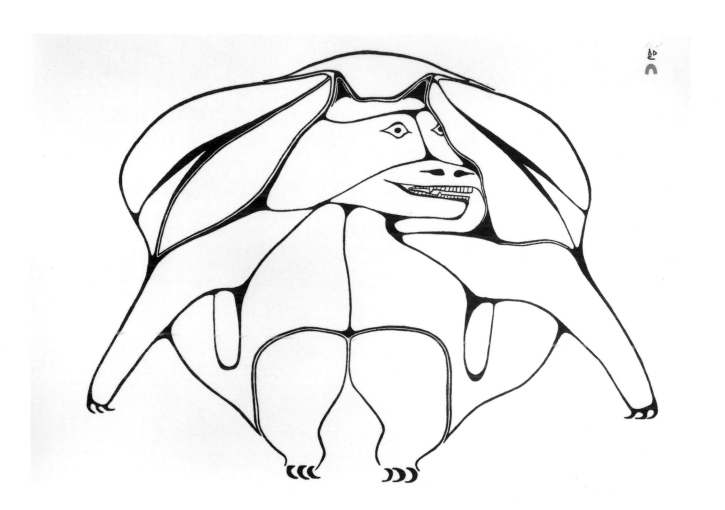

WOLF SPIRIT
1987
stonecut, 48/50
on wove, kozo paper
printed by *Iyola
Kingwatsiak*, 1933–
54.9 x 70.9 cm
Cape Dorset 1987,
no. 22

Amaruq *is a big thing. I
said I was just using
my imagination.
Amaruq, a wolf, is a big
animal. Dominant like
men, they go hunting
for wolves because they
are dominant, fierce.*
1992 interveiw with Marion E.
Jackson and Odette Leroux

FLIGHT OF FANTASY
1988
stonecut, 41/50
on laid, kozo paper
printed by *Iyola
Kingwatsiak*, 1933–
47.5 x 64.5 cm
Cape Dorset 1988,
no. 28

*That's also from my
own imagination that I
drew. I did not even
think of Pudlo, [he was]
my uncle.*
1991 interview with Odette
Leroux

SHELTERED OWL
1987
stonecut and stencil,
proof III (edition: 50)
on wove, kozo paper
printed by *Pee
Mikkigak*, 1940–
55.3 x 70.9 cm
Cape Dorset 1987,
no. 24

*This is the shade from
the wolf and the owl.
This is just imaginary
to me, like animation.*
1992 interview with Marion E.
Jackson and Odette Leroux

Red-necked Loon
1988
stonecut, proof II
(edition: 50)
on wove, kozo paper
printed by *Kavavau
Munamee*, 1958–
55.2 x 72.5 cm
Cape Dorset 1988,
no. 30

Changing Traditions   Lithograph   W.B.E.C. Proof II/IV   Dorset 1991   Pitaloosie

CHANGING
TRADITIONS
1991
lithograph, WBEC proof
II/IV (edition: 50)
on wove paper
watermark:
Arches/France
printed by *Pitseolak
Niviaqsi, 1947–*
57.4 x 66.2 cm
Cape Dorset 1991,
no. 20

*I did this as a litho-
graphic stone, and I
could move around. I
was looking at it from
one angle, but with my
other work I had to do
it from another angle.
That's why it has an
oblong look, because I
could move around on
a flat surface. This one
has a meaning, three
generations: my great-*

*grandmother, my
grandmother and my
mother. I just thought
of some generations
from pictures I saw.
Sealskin with long
skirts from that
time…. Like a fashion
show which I like. Not
generally what they
are wearing but the
excitement.*

1992 interview with Marion E.
Jackson and Odette Leroux

OWLS OF THE NIGHT
1990
lithograph, WBEC proof
II/III (edition: 50)
on wove, rag paper
printed by *Pitseolak*
Niviaqsi, 1947–
56.7 x 75.9 cm
Cape Dorset 1990,
no. 13

YOUNG LOONS
1990
lithograph, WBEC
proof II/IV (edition: 50)
on wove, rag paper
watermark:
Arches/France
printed by *Pitseolak*
Niviaqsi, 1947–
112.7 x 76.5 cm
Cape Dorset 1990,
no. 14

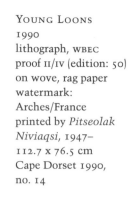

WOMAN PROUDLY
SEWING
1988
lithograph, proof II
(edition: 50)
on wove, rag paper
watermark:
Arches/France
printed by *Pitseolak
Niviaqsi, 1947–*
114 x 80.5 cm
Cape Dorset 1988,
no. 33

This is a woman, carrying a baby in her amauti and sewing. I enjoyed making it as it was the first time I ever made anything large from a [lithographic] stone. And I have always wondered why the artists don't ever make large drawings. Drawing on a larger piece of stone seems easier than making a drawing out of a smaller one.
Comment written by
Pitaloosie Saila in March 1991
on one of her favourite prints

Oopik Pitsiulak

I never fetched the water with a sealskin pot.
I usually fetch the water with a store-bought pot.
'Oopik Fetching Water.' I like that title because
although I was carrying the baby in my back,
I still had to go to get some water.

1992 interview with Marion E.
Jackson and Odette Leroux

Oopik Pitsiulak
1946–

Unlike most Inuit of her generation who grew up in camps on the land, Oopik Pitsiulak was raised in the small settlements near the Hudson's Bay Company trading posts in Lake Harbour and Cape Dorset. Several of her close relatives worked for the Hudson's Bay Company when she was a child, including her grandmother, her uncle, George Pitsiulak, with whom she lived for a number of years in Lake Harbour, and her father, Tommy Manning, who has managed the Hudson Bay Company store in Cape Dorset for many years. As a result of this upbringing, Oopik speaks English as well as Inuktitut and is comfortable with customs and technologies of the Euro-Canadian culture. Nevertheless, her own identity is clearly rooted in her own Inuit traditions from which she draws inspiration for her art and which she celebrates in her finely crafted sculptures.

Born in September, 1946, Oopik Pitsiulak spent the first nine years of her life in Lake Harbour where, following her mother's death, she was raised by her aunt and uncle, Nellie and George Pitsiulak. Oopik's grandmother, Simatuq, was an important influence in these early years. In 1955, Oopik moved to Cape Dorset to rejoin her father, Tommy Manning, who had by then married, Udluriak, daughter of the great south Baffin leader, Peter Pitseolak. Oopik's reunion with her father and his growing family and her relationship with her new grandfather, Peter Pitseolak, were to be a major influences in her life. She recalls that in the mid-1960s, she and others helped Peter Pitseolak with his carvings and that was what inspired her to try some carving on her own. In the traditional Inuit style of

arranged marriage, Oopik was married to Peter Pitseolak's adopted son, Mark Tapaungai, in 1964; that marriage dissolved in 1972. Oopik has five children.

Now coming into her own as an artist with a distinctive style and clear vision of her goals, Oopik Pitsiulak is beginning to integrate beadwork into her sculptural compositions, and she recalls with pride first learning beadwork in Lake Harbour from watching her grandmother. Oopik's stepmother, Udluriak, and Peter Pitseolak's wife, Aggeok, were also highly accomplished beadworkers, doing intricate beaded designs on the decorative *atigi* worn by traditional Inuit women over their warmer underclothing.

Oopik celebrates the strengths of traditional Inuit women in her art and often thinks of the strong women in her background and their sense for beauty when making her sculptures. Her work has been included in several group exhibitions of Inuit art including *Eskimo Canada*, Canadian Guild of Crafts Quebec and La Fédération des Coopératives du Nouveau-Québec (1968); *Sculpture/Inuit: Masterworks of the Canadian Arctic*, an exhibition organized by the Canadian Eskimo Arts Council that toured internationally (1971-1973); *Cape Dorset—Selected Sculpture from the Collection of the W.A.G.*, Winnipeg Art Gallery (1975); and *Die Kunst aus der Arktis*, organized by the Department of Indian and Northern Affairs, Canada, for exhibition in Mannheim and Frankfurt, West Germany (1985-86). Oopik Pitsiulak's work is also represented in important private and public collections including the Canadian Museum of Civilization; the Montréal Museum of Fine Arts; and the Winnipeg Art Gallery. She views the present as the beginning of a new phase in her artistic career and is enthusiastic about the new artistic directions she is currently exploring.

Things I Learned
from My Grandmother

Oopik Pitsiulak

I WAS BORN in the community of Lake Harbour and was raised there, not around camps. My mother was Elisapee, but everybody called her Pitsiulak. My father is Tommy Manning. He was working at that time for the Hudson's Bay Company in Lake Harbour and also at a camp outside Iqaluit called Iqaluijuik. We used to go visit the outpost camps by dog team. In the wintertime, the people from the camps would come into Lake Harbour to shop.

My mother died when I was a little girl. That was the year 1948. She had T.B. She died in a hospital in Halifax, Nova Scotia, and she is buried down there. It was that same year that my father came to Cape Dorset to work for the Hudson's Bay Company, and he left me behind in Lake Harbour. I don't remember my father leaving for Cape Dorset. He was working for the Hudson's Bay Company, and he came here to Cape Dorset. They had asked him to travel around the North to the other Hudson's Bay posts—Arctic Bay included—but he refused to go. He came to Cape Dorset because it was close, close to Lake Harbour so he could be near to his family.

Later in 1948, my father came back from Cape Dorset to Lake Harbour. He had already found a new wife, and he came back to Lake Harbour to get me and my sister, Ainiaq. When we were about ready to leave for Cape Dorset and were already in the peterhead boat, my aunt who had been raising me from the time my mother was taken down South could not part with me. I was already in the peterhead boat, but my aunt—my father's sister—could not part with me, so I stayed there. Nellie was her name. Nellie was looking after me and, during that time, Nellie and George Pitsiulak got together. I grew up with that family. George Pitsiulak worked for the Hudson's Bay Company, too.

I remember another time when my father and stepmother came from Cape Dorset to Lake Harbour on a dog team. They came to adopt Jimmy from my aunt, Nellie. I remember Jimmy because I was five years old at the time in 1951. I remember when Jimmy was born. I thought that someone cut my aunt open, and Jimmy came out. Because I was five years old, I thought that's what happened—cut her open, and out comes Jimmy! That was my belief about how babies were born.

Also, at the time of that visit I remember thinking, "Oh, that is what my father looks like and that is what my mother looks like." I remember my stepmother, Udluriak, speaking to me and asking me a question. She was saying, "Whom am I?" When I would not answer, Udluriak would say, "I'm your mother. I'm your mother, Udluriak." And then every time Udluriak asked the question, "Who am I to you?" I would say, "You're my mother." At that time, I was young enough to believe that she was my real mother. Then one time my father's younger brother, Joe Aluktut, told me—at that young age—"That's not your real mother." And his words stuck in my head. And I got very shy and embarrassed about that because I had gotten to think that Udluriak was my real mother. But my father's single brother told me, "That's not your real mother." And after that I don't remember. It seems like I fell asleep for three years.

I remember my grandmother, Simatuq. She was a cleaning lady for the Hudson's Bay Company. She wasn't just a cleaning lady. She did cooking and sewing and she did beadwork. She wasn't just a cleaning lady—she was a real woman. Because I learned beading from my grandmother, I am working at it today, and I like doing it very much. My grandmother did beading on parkas—like the trim along the cuffs of the sleeves and on the *atigi*. And my grandmother decorated my father's sisters' *amautiit* with beads and also with those big English things. I think they are called "sixpence." She used to put those down the back. And she made beaded pins, too. I want very much to make pins, beaded pins like my grandmother used to make. I don't have any right now. I am just on the way to seriously

doing beadwork. I am collecting my mind to doing beading.

There is another thing I remember from long ago about my grandmother. Down near Lake Harbour there is a place where you can catch cod fish. One time, my grandmother had pilot biscuits and she had cod and chopped it up into bits and pieces and added onions and put it inside a stove. She had pilot biscuits, cod and onions, and put this in an oven. I remember that from when I was a little girl because my grandmother did it. Up to that point, I could remember my grandmother. And after that point, that's when my grandmother died. But because I was seven years old, I was able to think and remember things, and I remember that my grandmother was very capable of doing a lot of things.

Another thing I remember is that there was a medical ship named *C.D. Howe*. My uncle and my aunt were put on that medical ship to go down South, and I came down here to Cape Dorset in 1955. That was Nellie and George Pitsiulak; they had T.B. and they went on the *C.D. Howe*. Because my aunt and my uncle were taken away, I came to be with my parents here in Cape Dorset. I cried very much when my aunt and my uncle left. Because they were my loved ones and they were taking them away, I cried and I didn't want them to go. They were taken away by a helicopter from the land to the ship. You would never know when those people who were taken away were going to come back. The planes going back and forth were very rare. Not knowing when they were coming back—or if ever—was very hard.

After that, I came to Cape Dorset, knowing that I was going to be growing up with my real family. That was like an extension on my life. After 1955, I started growing up with my real family—with my real sisters and brothers. The other part of my life, from 1955 on down, that was a different life, a different way of life with my aunt and uncle. I think I have had two lives! Thinking of families—a family is good if they have the

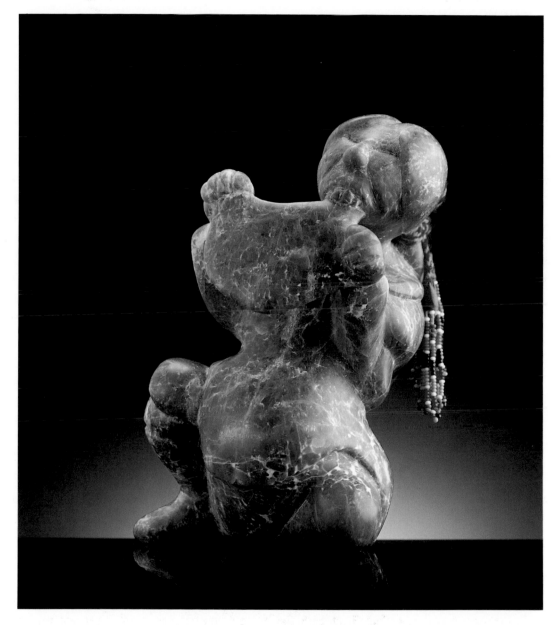

Oopik Softening
the Skin
1990
green stone, glass beads,
leather, wool cord and
synthetic cord
18.4 x 12.8 x 10.2 cm
signed
IV-C-5496

*I used to be like that…
with a baby in my
amauti, I'd chew the
skin. Yes, thinking of
myself.*

*Ever since I was a little
girl, I have chewed
sealskins. I started a
carving of a girl chew-
ing sealskin but it was
taken from outside our
house before I could
finish it. I had just
chipped the form of a
girl chewing sealskin
but it was taken. Since*

*then I've been thinking
of doing a similar one
because I've done that
as part of growing up,
up till now.*

*Oopik softening the
skin to be* kamiit.
1992 interview with Marion E.
Jackson and Odette Leroux

OOPIK THINKING
1990
dark green stone, glass
beads and wool cord
12.7 x 11.5 x 6.4 cm
unsigned
IV-C-5495

*Oopik sitting down and
thinking about what I
am going to carve next.
Because that is exactly
what I usually do first.*
1992 interview with Marion E.
Jackson and Odette Leroux

same values in life. When I was growing up with my aunt and uncle and they had all these kids, we would eat together as a group. We all would eat together, the whole big family. That is what it was like in Lake Harbour. When I came here to Cape Dorset, it was the same kind of family thing, with all of us together. Good feeling. Really together. And because Udluriak was very good at sewing, we always had warm clothing to wear. Because of our father, we had skins. Udluriak always sewed clothes for the kids. *Nunavut* is "cold"; *nunavut* means "our land." It's a cold place. And even though it is very cold, my stepmother always sewed clothing for us—for as many kids as there were plus our father. We always had warm clothing.

Udluriak was very much of a beadmaker too. I never saw her do any beading. But she always had beaded things she had made, lots of them. And Aggeok, Peter Pitseolak's wife, she always did beadwork, too. Too bad I never saw them beading. I always saw the beadwork all finished. My sister, Annie Manning, has little bits of that beadwork. My whole family was around me here in Cape Dorset. We all had the same father but different mothers, but we are family just the same.

The very first carving I ever did was over in R.C. Valley [the valley where the Roman Catholic mission once stood] in 1963. My very first carving was a female head, just a head. As I was doing that carving, Mark Pitseolak started coming toward me. I was carving near a little pond. When Mark Pitseolak started coming, I threw the carving in that pond. I was very shy, and we were just getting together at that time. Now I am so sorry! That was my very first carving.

The next year, I got married. It was an Inuktitut marriage—arranged. We got married 21 July, 1964. My husband was Mark Pitseolak. That is when I really started doing some carving. Mark Pitseolak was an adopted son to Peter Pitseolak, and Peter Pitseolak was a carver. Peter Pitseolak was my father-in-law, so I started helping him by filing and also sand-papering after he had finished his carvings, to help smooth them out. My husband started helping Peter Pitseolak with his carvings too, not just me. Then I decided I was going to start carving, too.

At that time, the Co-op was charging for soapstones. I bought a stone for ten bucks. I couldn't lift it, it was so big. So my husband carried it home for me, and I carved it. The very first carving I did was a woman—woman with a baby on her back in an *amauti*. After I finished it, my husband carried it back for me. It was really heavy. I got $110 for it, and I paid the $10 out of that $110. That one in 1967 was my first one that I got money from, that one of that woman. After that time, I started carving birds, seals, fish, whales. I used to like doing *ukpiit* a lot. That was at that time, but I do not make too many *ukpiit* now.

Because everybody was making seals and fish and everyday things that they see and that they could easily carve, I wanted to do something different. If I think about something—like my carvings—then I think about it and want to make my thought a reality. I think, and my thoughts have to come out. I make my thoughts a reality in my carvings. For me, carving is not just a way to get money. It is a way of expressing myself and making myself understood. I like the carvings I have done. I have kids now and grandchildren. They are going to be growing up, and they are going to see these things. I don't carve all the time, only rarely. Recently, I have been re-arranging my mind for doing more carvings and expressing myself.

In my life, I have had many experiences. One of the most meaningful was when I finished my carving of myself [*Oopik Going For Water*] with beadwork like my grandmother used to make. When I finished that carving, I took it to the Co-op. I think it had been sent down South already when Jimmy [Manning, Assistant Manager of the West Baffin Co-operative] said to me, "You really put yourself into this—your full physical and mental self," as if to say, "I am proud of you." I will always remember that. It really touched me. Being the Co-op person, Jimmy receives a lot of carvings, and he doesn't just take them. He tells a person, "You could improve here," and "You could do this." If a carving could have been done better, he says that.

Recently, I was with the Inuit organization called *Pauttuutit* [the Inuit Women's Association based in Ottawa]. They were meeting in Kuujjuaq last week, and I was part of that group. A lot of the women were expressing themselves very openly to other women. And I was part of that. My reason for talking about this group is that I started to see how women think, how they have an artistic way of forming things, like carvings, sewing, any female art—any way of sewing, traditional clothing. That's what I started realizing: that women have real important roles. That was when I realized that women can do a lot. Women are very capable. They have been very capable for a long time, but it is just now that their capabilities are coming out in the open. I was proud to be part of that women's group because it made me realize that women are good, that women are strong. I think if my grandmother were alive, she would be proud too because she was very capable.

Putting up the Tent   lithograph   23/50   Dec

Mayoreak ᒪᔪᕆᐊ

Mayoreak Ashoona

She likes putting up tents.
This woman is putting up a new tent....
   Some of the strings are not hitched yet, since they are alternated....
  The woman is wearing modern clothes
  and is carrying some rocks for the tent.

1991 interview with
Odette Leroux

Mayoreak Ashoona
1946–

More than most Inuit women of her generation, Mayoreak Ashoona remains immersed in the traditional experience of her culture. Though she and her husband, Qaqaq Ashoona, lived in Cape Dorset for more than fifteen years during the 1960s and 1970s, they returned to the land in the late 1970s and live today with their youngest son and two adopted grandsons at Shatureetuk, an isolated outpost camp on South Baffin Island. Mayoreak was born in this same camp in 1946. Her mother was Sheouak Parr (1923—1961), one of the first women to begin making drawings to support the experimental efforts at printmaking in Cape Dorset in the late 1950s. Mayoreak's childhood and young adult years were spent on the land following the traditional Inuit lifestyle. Shatureetuk was her family's main camping area, though she remembers travelling among various South Baffin camps including Ittiliakjuk, Ikirashaq, Igalallik and Qarmaajuk and finding "everything exciting." Although today Mayoreak and Qaqaq Ashoona have a small frame house and a short-wave radio at Shatureetuk, they are an hour's journey by snowmobile from Cape Dorset and they follow much of the lifestyle of an earlier generation. Qaqaq hunts and teaches the skills of hunting to his son and grandchildren, and Mayoreak takes pride in preparing skins, sewing clothing, and preparing and storing meat and fish using methods she learned from her mother.

Both Mayoreak and Qaqaq are prominent Inuit artists and use their art to express both values and experiences of the traditional Inuit culture. Mayoreak's drawings, like her husband's sculpture, depict the activities that have given shape and meaning to their lives. Mayoreak often draws birds or Arctic animals and Inuit engaged in traditional activities, particularly those activities that involve women or the communal efforts of family groups. Mayoreak and Qaqaq became involved in art independently and have developed their own clearly recognizable styles. Perhaps not coincidentally, Mayoreak and Qaqaq are also both offspring of prominent early Cape Dorset artists. Mayoreak's mother, Sheouak, was one of the first women to respond to James Houston's request for drawings in the late 1950s, and Sheouak's abstracted human figure design is still in use as a logo for the West Baffin Eskimo Co-operative. Mayoreak can remember Sheouak beginning to draw at Shatureetuk. Though Qaqaq's mother, Pitseolak Ashoona, also resided briefly at Shatureetuk at that time, it was not until Pitseolak moved permanently into Cape Dorset that she began to draw, becoming eventually one of the most prolific and respected Inuit artists of her generation.

Though Mayoreak began drawing at Shatureetuk herself in the early 1960s, she has had periods of prolific drawing and intermittent periods when family responsibilities have not allowed time for her art. Since 1978 when Mayoreak's images first appeared in the Cape Dorset print collection, a total of thirty-five of her works have been included in annual collections and she has been represented each year since 1978 except 1988 and 1992. Mayoreak's graphic works have also been included in several exhibitions featuring work by Inuit artists, among them: *Cape Dorset 1978 Collection of Twenty-six Lithographs*, Canadian Guild of Crafts Quebec (1978); *Inuit Art in the 1970s*, Agnes Etherington Art Centre, Kingston (1979-80); *The Inuit Amautik: I Like My Hood To Be Full*, Winnipeg Art Gallery (1980); *Return of the Birds*, Vancouver Art Gallery (1983); *Chisel and Brush / Le ciseau et la brosse*, touring exhibition organized by the Department of Indian Affairs and Northern Development (1985-87); and *Northern Exposure: Inuit Images of Travel*, Burnaby Art Gallery, Burnaby, (1986). Her art is also included in the permanent collections of the Canadian Museum of Civilization; the Inuit Cultural Institute, Rankin Inlet; the National Gallery of Canada, Ottawa; the Prince of Wales Northern Heritage Centre, Yellowknife; and the Winnipeg Art Gallery.

---

facing overleaf:
PUTTING UP THE TENT
1982
lithograph, 22/50
on wove, rag paper
watermark:
Arches/France

printed by *Pitseolak Niviaqsi*, 1947–
51.5 x 66.7 cm
Cape Dorset 1982,
no. LI9

My Life at Shatureetuk

Mayoreak Ashoona

I WAS BORN on 22 September, 1946, at Shatureetuk where my parents lived and I am still living today. I am now forty-seven years old and have five children still living. My oldest, Mary, is now twenty-nine; Kuluk, another daughter, is twenty-three; the child I had after Kuluk died; my son Siasi is twenty-one; Ottokie is nineteen; Komwartok is sixteen; and I am raising two grandsons, Ningeocheak, twelve, and Sappa, eight years old. Some of my children now have children of their own while some are still not married. My husband, children and I are the only ones living at Shatureetuk. All of my children grew up at our camp in Shatureetuk.

While I was a young child growing up at Shatureetuk, I remember my mother telling us to respect our parents and the traditional way of life always. I will never forget my parents' words of wisdom. My mother knew my grandfather's way of life, and she told me those stories. From her, I am fortunate to know the culture and the traditional way of the Inuit. I will always make the Inuit things that I was taught as long as I am able. I will never forget the Inuktitut terms that I use for everything; everything has a name. I could write on and on about my way of life, about what I enjoy doing, and about what I know.

I try to teach all of my children how to live their lives sensibly and about the Inuit way of life. I always tell them the Inuit terms for things, which things are edible, and the steps for making things so that they can make them themselves. Some of my children make their own things now and can read in Inuktitut. Some of my children know both Inuktitut and English. One of my sons makes carvings out of soapstone, and so do my daughters once in a while. I have always encouraged my children to try to make things; even my youngest makes carvings.

I started making carvings to make an income at our outpost camp. I did not want to just sit around doing nothing, so I started thinking of what I could do to help my husband

SHORE BIRDS
1978
lithograph, 19/50
on wove, rag paper
printed by *Aoudla
Pudlat, 1951–*
51.7 x 66.8 cm
Cape Dorset 1978,
no. L2

*I tried to get the shape
to resemble a bird as it
looks. And I created
the colours out of my
own imagination,
although I have never
seen a bird the way I
coloured them. I
coloured the beak that
way I like the colour to
mix. Just for my experi-
ment with the colours.
The reason why I put
those rocks there, is
that some birds sit in
rocky areas. The edge
of the lake usually has
some rocky areas,
that's where some
birds do sit. I often see
birds like seagulls,
loons, the seabirds eat-
ing a fish. All the birds
are meant to eat the
fish. There is one with
a fish and the rest are
waiting to be fed.*
1991 interview with Odette
Leroux

financially. My mother had always told me to try to make things when I grew up. I have even learned how to make men's things. I have always tried to do things that could strengthen my muscles; I try to have a healthy body and mind. I do all these things without being lazy because we have a Helper whom we cannot see. I am happy when we have completed what we had set out to do at our camp.

Living in an outpost camp, you have to know and understand the Inuit way of life. My mother used to teach me how to do things and make different things by telling me and showing me until I remembered, like showing me how to prepare skins. There are some things that I had to learn on my own, like sewing, because my mother died before she could teach me. I also remember what my father used to tell me about life. Even if you're a female, there are times when you try to catch animals for food. This is what I do out at the outpost camp, with a rifle or even without one. Following traditional ways, I try to catch ptarmigan by throwing stones at them and to fish with sticks that are sharpened, rather than using a rod or string. Sometimes, though, I use a hook and line.

During the winter, summer, spring, and fall months, I continue living the traditional way of the Inuit. During the winter months, if the weather is good, both my husband and I go fishing every day. I stop fishing when the lake ice becomes too thick. Then I start doing other things at home—carving, drawing and making clothing, and also cleaning house inside and on the porch. I also help my husband with things that need to be done. On Sundays I take time off to rest. Then the next day, on Monday, I get back to my everyday chores.

Every year, I prepare skins, sew clothing, make soapstone carvings, and I have also been drawing since the time they started buying drawings. I will put all of my abilities towards what needs doing, as long as my abilities are available to me. There are times when it is very difficult if I've not yet learned how to do something. But, as we are the only ones living at our outpost camp, I do get things done! There has never been anyone there to answer my questions, so I've had to learn how to do things and make things on my own. I had started learning how to do the things a woman does when I was a young girl, and I haven't stopped wanting to learn on my own how to make things.

During the winter, I prepare sealskins, but as they are frozen then, I first have to thaw them out. I wash the blood out of the skins with sea water while the tide is low because that is the best way to take care of the skin and fur. Since the sea is not always dependable, I sometimes have to go to the shoreline to wash them out. I also go trapping for fox around our camp, and if there are fox, I catch some. I take along my children— Sappa, Ningeocheak and Komwartok—to teach them how to set traps. So far they have done well.

I have known the Inuit traditional ways of survival ever since I was taught them. I know about camping while out hunting and about making an igloo, and during summertime, about hunting on foot, even if there is no tent handy. My husband has taught me what things to do and how to do them whenever I have gone along with him. As women, we don't know everything that men do to survive, so we do need to be told. In the same manner, the men do not know everything that women do to take care of things, so we have to teach them. I have tried to put down the honest truth about what it is like to live in the Arctic. I have tried to teach about the land and the weather conditions and about what to do inside the house. These are the things that I do.

As to the food we keep outside the house, the country food, this can only be cut up with an axe because it is frozen solid. If my husband does not take the food in, I have to bring it in, and if the meat is too frozen, I have to thaw it out or get it thawed enough to cut. Once the meat is thawed out enough to cut, I cook it. There are also times when I have to wait to have my meal because of urgent things that need tending. That is how it is because I am the only female in our camp. There is always plenty to do when you live in an outpost camp. The only time I take time off is on Sundays if I am too tired. Those are the many things I have to do here.

I dry the clothes outdoors as well because they dry out better that way, until the weather becomes too cold. If they are put outdoors to dry when it is too cold, they could be ruined. That includes drying animal hides; they can only be dried during the springtime. There is a time to do everything, and that is what I do, always making sure I know what the weather is good for. When it comes to drying sealskins, I make sure that they will turn out all right, tending to them day by day. I always make sure that they are put in the shade away from direct sunlight so that the skins will be a nice white colour. I make sure, too, of the things that I am drying indoors, so that they do not become ruined and so that when I make things they'll turn out nicely.

If the caribou leg skins are available, I prepare them by softening the skins and making the skin white. I also clean the caribou sinews and dry them out because they come in handy as thread during the winter. I also go along with my husband during the spring to get caribou skins, while the hair on the caribou skin is not too thick. The thinner-haired caribou skin is made into the leggings of women's *kamiit*. The leggings of men's *kamiit* are made out of skin from caribou legs when the caribou are caught during the summer. The caribou skins aren't as good during the spring season for making into leggings for *kamiit*. As long as they're available, the skins of the caribou caught during the winter are made into mittens, and on some skins I'll remove the hair if I want.

I use both the skins and the meat from the animals caught around our area as they become available. I am the only one who prepares the food in our camp while my husband works.

Even if I, too, am working on something else, I still take time to prepare the family meals as there isn't anyone else I could ask to help me out. Also, there are always dishes to wash.

One time, I went by dog team from Shatureetuk to Cape Dorset with my grandchildren, Ningeocheak and Sappa, to purchase more food before we completely ran out. I had to return to our camp before nightfall while the weather was still favourable and because my husband had stayed behind. I have travelled alone to Cape Dorset and back without my husband during the winter and summer months.

I have written down some of the things I do at our camp, and some of the things I do can be done any time as they are the Inuit way of life. I have always lived this way of life for as long as I can remember. During the winter, it is a tradition to go out to the floe edge to collect *kuanniq*, so my husband takes me out. That is another of the things I do at the camp.

What I find takes the most time is making drawings because you have to think of something to draw. In life out at the camp, I find that there are so many other things that need to be done, whether it be fetching water, cleaning house or sewing. I have been making drawings for a long time. These are the things that I do.

For some of the things I make, you have to make sure you know how to make them; some things take quite a long time to complete while others do not take so long. When I make clothing and when I make things that I get paid for, I do not take the task lightly nor do I go through the tasks at a single stretch. I first have to make a decision on what to make and how to do it. Then I finally start. When I have finally completed what I set out to make, I am happy. Whatever I have decided to make, like women's utensils, I make them in my imagination first, thinking how I would like them to be, how they could be improved. I create my own designs on clothing that I sew for the winter season, such as *kamiik* and mittens.

I also know how to make Inuit toys for children. For both boys and girls, I make a toy called *ajagak* out of Arctic hares' skulls, seal bones and ptarmigan crops when they're available. I also go fishing at the lake with my children on foot; we use rocks to make the fish visible, then use sticks with lines to harpoon them during the summertime.

At our camp in Shatureetuk, I have to fetch ice for water with a small sled as water is not delivered to us. During the summer, with my children's help, I clean up the garbage that has accumulated around our camp, then burn it. I also burn the garbage during the winter. I wash all our laundry by hand. After all the chores are done, sometimes I'll sit down to read the Bible to learn more how I should be living my life.

I also go into the Cape Dorset settlement by dog team to fetch medication from the nursing station for my husband when he runs out or when he becomes ill. Then I'll go back to my carving or sewing, then later I'll go back to my drawings, always making sure I have decided how best to prepare our meals. When it is time to go about making them, first I'll clean and tidy up the house. On Sundays, I'll go outside for walks while I have time off. Then I'll tend to our lighting supplies before it gets dark, so we can have light in our home in the evening. Once in a while, too, I'll call Cape Dorset to check and see if my children [who live there] are all right. When I do go see them, I make sure that I bring country food for them. I have to make sure that they do not go hungry so I bring them food; sometimes the younger ones will come with me when I go. When I do make it to Cape Dorset once in a while, I am thankful to both the Inuit and the *qallunaat* for making me welcome. I always leave my children a bit of pocket money if I have any left over before heading back to Shatureetuk.

At Shatureetuk, I make my carvings only with an axe and a file, with no electric tools, and with only my grandchildren and my husband for company. I make all our clothes from caribou skins. I use all of the animal skins to make what we need such as clothing, depending on how the weather is during the winter, summer and spring. During the summer I prepare the skins to make clothing out of later on, depending on if the weather is still good for drying them. I do not take lightly the preparation of the skins: my husband and I always make sure that we dry them properly and set them aside. During the coldest months of the winter, I do not dry the animal skins, because that will wreck them. I also dry the skins outside during the spring while it is still light out, but protect them from direct sunlight. That is how I take care of the animal skins; that is expected of a woman at home. I am responsible for the sewing, cleaning our home, cooking the meals as well as visiting my children at Cape Dorset by dog team if the weather is favourable.

Also, if my husband is going hunting I go along, but there are also times I will go off hunting on the land on my own, never out at the sea during the winter. Every summer, I go along to Kangisujuak by boat, and of course we try and make sure that our belongings for making money are kept in good repair as they aren't always handy to get when you need them. We try and make sure that we have enough gas for the outboard. I try and make sure that I know about these things as I'm the only woman in our camp.

I make whatever I know how to make, and some things I figure out how to make on my own from what is available to us at the time. What stands in my way is my lack of knowledge of the *qallunaat* language, though there are a few simple words I do understand. The words I know in Inuktitut I will never forget as long as I live the traditional way of life. I tend to the duties expected of me as a woman in a traditional sense, and I try and make some of the traditional tools that the Inuit have had. I also try to teach my children while I make different things. I make clothing out of animal skins because I find that they are the most useful on land during the fall and spring seasons.

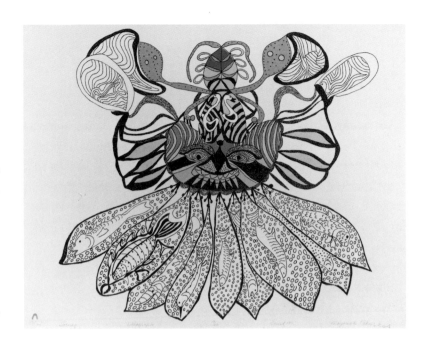

Tornaq
1977
lithograph, 19/50
on wove, rag paper
printed by *Aoudla
Pudlat, 1951–*
52 x 67.7 cm
Cape Dorset 1978,
no. L3

I dreamt of something that had some animals inside a glass…. They are fish that I saw in the water, different species, so I drew the pictures from my memory using my imagination.
1991 interview with Odette Leroux

Once I have made the clothing, I start tending to other things. All of the things that need to be taken care of have to be done with care. I do all of those things as well as trying to make sure I know what is going on outdoors in case I might see an animal or another human being. You really have to be aware of everything around you, because the weather is not always predictable. I have led people into our home who would otherwise have frozen to death. I dry off their clothing and feed them. Those are the things that I do.

I have always wished I could be paid more for the things I make to sell that were valuable in our traditional culture. When I think I have made enough things, my husband and I go and try to sell them. I would like to be able to make money from selling things I can make out of caribou and sealskins instead of selling the drawings I make about those things. Those are some of the ideas I have on how I could make money, because I make clothing for us already at home. I do my drawings and carve all day at times, even though I am tired and especially if I have a lot of papers to make my drawings on. I try not to get too worked up if I get overloaded with things to do on top of everyday chores. There are times when it is hard because I have the cooking, cleaning and sewing to do as well. If my husband is away, I try to get as much done as possible before he arrives back home, because when he returns I have to help him with what needs doing.

I have written down how I live my life at Shatureetuk, our outpost camp. I can do all the things that I have learned by following the Inuit traditional way of life. Trying to improve things that I make to make them more useful, I do not just make things without care. Everything is done with care. From the time I was a young girl to now, my sewing technique has changed. I soften up the *kamiit* I have made on a stretcher made of wooden sticks. The caribou skins I soften with a softening tool. I do not make only one set of clothes; I have to make several at a time. I make three inner caribou coats so I have different caribou skins that need to be prepared first. I also have to prepare the sealskins by myself. I also use the skins for other things after drying them, for cleaning things as well.

I also make our tent using a sewing machine. I make sure that the bedding that we use is in good repair, and fetch firewood as well. Sometimes my husband will take me by boat to search for firewood and bedding if we should be on an island where there isn't firewood already handy. I also use rocks for the bedding area and for the floor area of the tent. I tend to these things carefully. A long time has passed now since the time I started living this way of life. I was a young girl, and it was before my children were born.

During 1961 I started drawing, when Tiuli [Terrence Ryan] started managing the craft shop. Then in 1962, I started carving. I have always enjoyed making carvings. I take my carvings to the Co-op. But what I have found is that if you have other things to take care of, it takes more time to do drawings, to draw them properly with a clear mind. My carvings, too, I make during the wintertime with only an axe as a tool. These are the things I do year-round—all winter, summer, spring and fall at our camp.

I have tried to put down everything that I do in the traditional Inuit way of life as I have lived it. Some of the things I do are what I learned from my mother by watching her as she taught me. She died when I was sixteen years of age, so what I learned after that time was self-taught.

FIRST GOOSE HUNT
1979
lithograph, 3/50
on wove, rag paper
printed by *Pitseolak
Niviaqsi*, 1947–
51.4 x 66.4 cm
Cape Dorset 1979,
no. L17

*It is usually exciting to
hunt birds. This person
here is supposed to
represent real-life hunt-
ing…. The birds (are)
representing a bird type
from the North.*
1991 interview with Odette
Leroux

BEAR SPIRIT
1979
lithograph, 7/50
on wove, rag paper
printed by *Aoudla
Pudlat*, 1951–
50.9 x 66 cm
Cape Dorset 1979,
no. L16

*I am poor at making
bears. There are also
two heads of a bird I
drew out of my imagi-
nation.*
1991 interview with Odette
Leroux

PUTTING UP
THE TENT
1981
lithograph, 48/50
on wove, rag paper
printed by *Pitseolak
Niviaqsi*, 1947–
54.8 x 66 cm
Cape Dorset 1981,
no. L19

*I like to set up the tent
when I am camping.
Those blankets or
clothing by the tent
will stay there until the
tent is set up. This is
exactly how I set up a
tent, even the pot is
ready to brew tea after
I put up the tent.*
1991 interview with Odette
Leroux

CLEANING FISH
1981
lithograph, 48/50
on wove, rag paper
watermark: BFK
Rives/France
printed by *Aoudla
Pudlat*, 1951–
56.4 x 71.3 cm
Cape Dorset 1981,
no. L20

*Some of it still exists,
as with the preparation
of the fish in order to
dry out, and then tie
them on the antlers
since there was no
wood back then. That's
a sealskin tent back
there.*
1991 interview with Odette
Leroux

DANCE OF THE WALRUS SPIRIT
1982
stonecut and stencil,
43/50
on laid, kozo paper
printed by *Saggiaktok Saggiaktok, 1932–*
63.1 x 69.5 cm
Cape Dorset 1982,
no. 34

The face is an owl, the body is a walrus. I drew it that way in order to make it look nice, although it was drawn to resemble plants.... I tried to draw pictures that do not resemble other peoples' drawings.... When I completed that draw-

ing, I thought that the owl became a walrus, since the feathers are coming off.
1991 interview with Odette Leroux

THE NEW KAMIKS
1982
stonecut and stencil,
43/50
on laid, kozo paper
printed by *Timothy
Ottochie, 1904–82*
62.5 x 50.3 cm
Cape Dorset 1982,
no. 32

*The drawing represents
a woman who has just
finished making some
kamiik and is just
about to stretch them
with a stretcher. I have
always had those
stretchers even up to
today. My husband
makes those kamiit
stretchers. That one is
stretching after having
the sinew put in. Those
are my needles and
muscle which came out
of a caribou. We use
that for sinew.*

*[We use a stretcher] to
widen the kamiit after
they shrink. As women,
when we complete our
work we get excited, so
we show our finished
material. I also like
women with braided
hair, that is why I drew
that picture with a
woman with long,
braided hair. And I am
a lady with long hair.*

1991 interview with Odette
Leroux

PREPARING SKINS
FOR KAYAK
1982
stonecut and stencil,
43/50
on laid, kozo paper
printed by *Pee
Mikkigak, 1940–*
55.8 x 75.2 cm
Cape Dorset 1982,
no. 33

*I drew that drawing
from hearing my father
talk about the proce-
dures they used to use
when they were getting
a skin ready for a
kayak. Or if they were
making tents, they
would hang them on a
piece of wood and use a
needle to sew as they
were hanging…. Square
flipper seal, bearded
seal…. They're sewing
the skins as they are
using their mouths to
chew the skin, in order
to moisten the skin….
The women who sew
these sealskins, other
people would collect
some plants, leaves
from the ground. In
order for the women to
chew, so that they*

*could sew it better. My
father used to tell sto-
ries about the old days
before some things they
use now existed. I
made sure I didn't lose
what I was taught from
my father…. There are
leaves on the ground in
the Arctic, but I can't
remember the precise
name of them…. [They
chew these leaves
because] the material
they were working on
would have to be total-
ly waterproof…. They
don't do this today. If
somebody wanted to do
this today, I am sure
somebody would be
able to demonstrate
how it is done.*

1991 interview with Odette
Leroux

CARIBOU
IN THE DISTANCE
1980
lithograph, 24/50
on wove, rag paper
printed by *Pitseolak
Niviaqsi, 1947–*
50.5 x 66.5 cm
Cape Dorset 1980,
no. L18

*This is a true-life exam-
ple of what has hap-
pened to me before.
Even the way they
carry the things is real
to how they used to
hike inland in search of
caribou. I saw this
scenery before, that's
why I put it in.*
1991 interview with Odette
Leroux

ANIMALS CONVERGE
1984
stonecut and stencil,
proof (edition: 50)
on wove, kozo paper
printed by *Lukta
Qiatsuk*, 1928–
49.3 x 64.6 cm
Cape Dorset 1984,
no. 18

*I have seen mountain
goats in books or T.V. I
liked the way the horns
curled so I drew it....
Birds are attracted to
animals without wings,
so the birds are watch-
ing the mountain
goats.... That is a raven,
a seagull, and the one
in the middle is an
Arctic tern. These are
the flippers of a walrus.*
1991 interview with Odette
Leroux

FISHERBIRDS
1984
stonecut, proof
(edition: 50)
on wove, kozo paper
printed by *Pee
Mikkigak*, 1940–
43.5 x 56.5 cm
Cape Dorset 1984,
no. 19

*I drew this because the
fish-eating birds who
have large and long
beaks, I interpreted
that the birds are scary
to fish. It has a fish
pouch to store them.
They are mates.*
1991 interview with Odette
Leroux

FAMILY OF FISHERMEN
1983
stonecut and stencil,
49/50
on laid, kozo paper
printed by *Eegyvudluk
Pootoogook, 1931–*
61.4 x 74.5 cm
Cape Dorset 1983,
no. 21

*I really enjoy going out
fishing and I often go
fishing. I [have] never
seen huge fish, but the
way I did them is to
show how much I enjoy
fishing.... That is hus-
band and wife both
with a fish, since my
husband and I both
like fishing. When I was*

*drawing this picture I
was thinking of my
husband and myself.*
1991 interview with Odette
Leroux

RAVEN OF
SHARTOWEETOK
1983
(Original title: *Owl of
Shartoweetok*. Changed
by artist.)
stonecut and stencil,
49/50
on laid, kozo paper
printed by *Saggiaktok
Saggiaktok, 1932–*
31.5 x 43 cm
Cape Dorset 1983,
no. 20

*Shartoweetok
(Shatureetuk) has a lot
of flat rocks and some
of them are pretty large
in size. That is why it
was named like that.
They're all over the
place, even on the
cliffs…. I usually watch
the owl and the raven;
it came from my imagi-
nation.*
1991 interview with Odette
Leroux and 1992 interview with
Marion E. Jackson and Odette
Leroux

*I add designs to this
one in order to make it
appealing. The raven is
carrying the owl in the
back. This one is not
an owl, I [drew] as a
raven…. The raven and
owls usually get mad
at each other. That is
what this appearance
resembles.*
1991 interview with Odette
Leroux

WALRUS ISLAND
1982
lithograph, 29/50
on wove, rag paper
printed by *Pitseolak
Niviaqsi, 1947–*
43.5 x 58.4 cm
Cape Dorset 1982,
no. L18

*The lithograph repre-
sents squirting water,
because walruses eat
clams and clams squirt
water…. They are back-
ward… on a reef… and
are ready to eat clams.*
1991 interview with Odette
Leroux

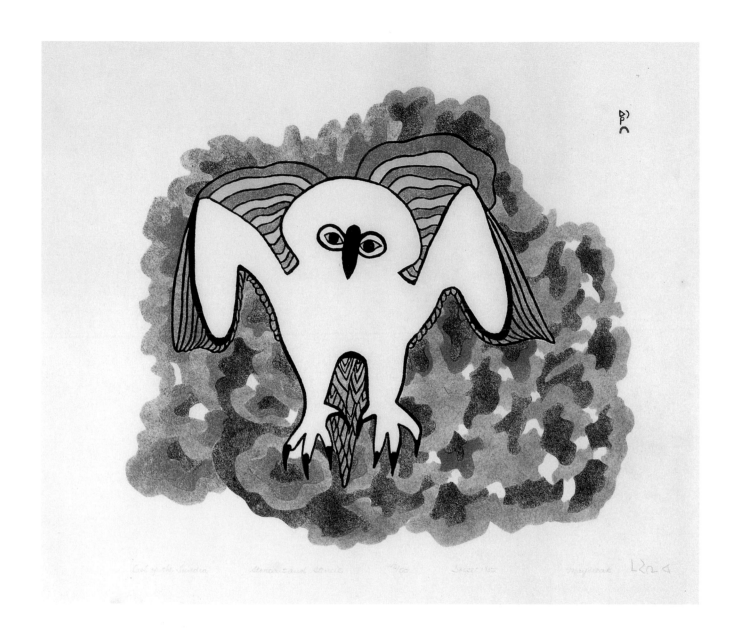

OWL OF THE TUNDRA
1982
stonecut and stencil,
43/50
on laid, kozo paper
printed by *Timothy
Ottochie, 1904–82*
62.6 x 69.5 cm
Cape Dorset 1982,
no. 35

*It is to represent a baby
owl…. The blue area is
to represent water, to
show that the owl is
not a water fowl.*
1991 interview with Odette
Leroux

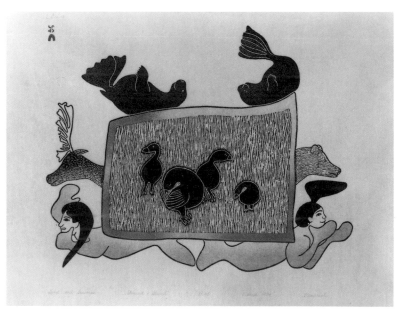

LAND AND SEASCAPE
1984
stonecut and stencil,
proof (edition: 50)
on wove, kozo paper
printed by *Saggiaktok
Saggiaktok, 1932–*
63.5 x 79.5 cm
Cape Dorset 1984,
no. 20

*I was thinking that
there are all kinds of
animals that I have
seen except for those
two [sea goddess or
mermaid].... I mixed
them together these
with birds, because
they cannot fly but the
birds can fly away....
The wind is blowing
her hair away.*
1991 interview with Odette
Leroux

WALRUS WATCH
NEWBORN
1984
stonecut and stencil,
proof (edition: 50)
on wove, kozo paper
printed by *Eegyvudluk
Pootoogook, 1931–*
60.5 x 73.9 cm
Cape Dorset 1984,
no. 21

*Those two are mates
carrying their babies
away on the ice.*
1991 interview with Odette
Leroux

FLIGHT OVER
FISH LAKE
1987
stonecut and stencil,
47/50
on wove, kozo paper
printed by *Laisa
Qajurajuk, 1935–*
55.5 x 61.5 cm
Cape Dorset 1987,
no. 18

*These two are brother
and sister, they were
taken away by the big
bird.... When I was
young I used to wish to
fly, so when I drew this,
I thought about how it
would be to fly with a
bird.*
1991 interview with Odette
Leroux

SEAGULL EATING
CHAR
AT THE RIVER
1989
green stone
57 x 8 x 27.9 cm
signed
IV-C-5483

Nocturnal Raven   Stonecut & Stencil   WBEC Proof I/V   Dorset 1989   Mayoreak

NOCTURNAL FALCON
1989
(Original title:
Nocturnal Raven.
Changed by artist.)
stonecut and stencil,
WBEC proof I/V
(edition: 50)
on wove, rag paper
watermark:
Arches/France

printed by *Pee
Mikkigak, 1940–*
55.2 x 67.3 cm
Cape Dorset 1989,
no. 17

*This took me quite a
while to do the work on
the little details to
make the many differ-
ent colours. The way I
have observed the fal-
cons when they are*
*ready to fly off from the
ground—they can even
twist their heads look-
ing right behind. It's
both the owl and falcon
can look back without
moving the body but
the head. Their bodies
would look bigger, as if
they got more air into
their bodies.*
1991 interview with Odette
Leroux

Two Arctic Murres
1987
lithograph, proof III
(edition: 50)
on wove, rag paper
printed by *Pitseolak
Niviaqsi, 1947–*
49.2 x 51.5 cm
Cape Dorset 1987,
no. 19

*They are representing
the murres' nesting
ground on an island
cliff.*
1991 interview with Odette
Leroux

Sharpening the Ulu
1989
stonecut, 47/50
on laid, kozo paper
printed by *Kavavau
Munamee, 1958–*
49 x 62 cm
Cape Dorset 1989,
no. 16

*This is a method that I
still use, skinning hides
in the wintertime. They
used to hang frozen
skins in order to melt,
but we still do them in
real life…. My mother
used to work on the
skins with the baby on
her* amauti, *so this is
the image of a woman
like my mother who*

*would do her work on
the skins. I even do
that now…. I would do
the cleaning and dry
the skins only during
the springtime, but not
frozen. I too would
carry the baby in my
amauti.*
1991 interview with Odette
Leroux

INNIUTIK
(DRYING RACK)
1990–91
green and grey stone,
caribou antler, sealhide,
thong, wood, paint and
bone
82 x 80.5 x 87 cm
signed
IV-C-5485 a-o

It is my sculpture of the skin thawing out on the rack just like my parents used to do. That sculpture is in reality the way my parents used to live.
1992 interview with Marion E. Jackson and Odette Leroux

These ones on the top are drying nets and pegs. On the top of the nets are drying stuffs, like mittens, socks, covers. The seal-oil lamps are usually used in the igloos, so there is the ordinary seal-oil lamp down there. It's the only main way of heating, cooking and making drinking water from ice that we used to have. The container under the seal-oil lamp is used for dripping old oil from the lamp. The moss would be drained with the tin can that has many little holes so you would make home-made wicks for the lamp. I was born before the Inuit started to use the primus stove.

So, whenever my father was going away hunting, he used to bring moss and also frozen seal oil ready to use and the moss would be soaked in the seal oil ready to use for the lamp to boil some water and to cook....

I was brought up living in igloos during the winter. When we were going near the floe edge we used to have igloos made to stay overnight....

A lamp stick, ulu, scraper, sharpener. Those are the things usually set by the right side of the woman's corner to be out of the reach....

Also the kamiit *and outer caribou parka. Actually anything that was wet. There were two types of nets, one would be a drying above the lamp with the pegs and the other one poked into the snow inside the igloo....*

I even used to see them used, but I never had to use one.
Quotes from a meeting on 7 March, 1991, of the artist with Minnie Aodla Freeman and Odette Leroux at Cape Dorset.

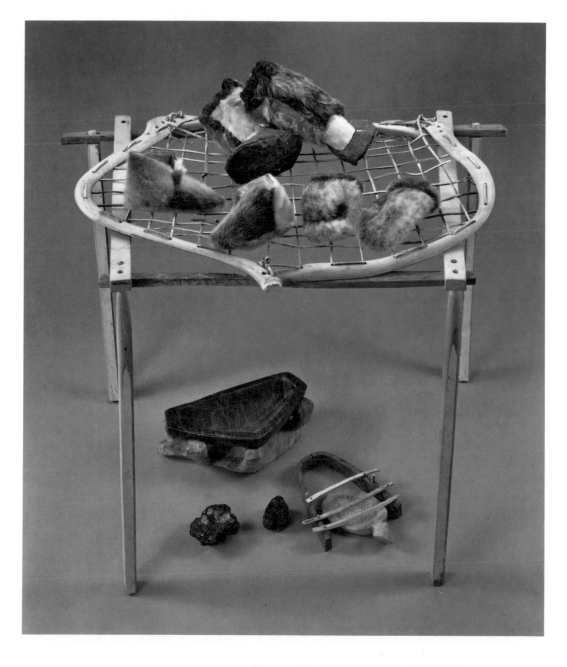

Ovilu Tunnillie

He is appearing from the ground
like the shaman would do...
the shaman were powerful to do impossible things.
A Shaman Appeared.

1992 interview with Marion E.
Jackson and Odette Leroux

Ovilu Tunnillie
1949–

Born in 1949 in the camp Kangia, Ovilu Tunnillie spent her earliest years with her parents growing up in the traditional Inuit lifestyle. Her father, Toonoo Toonoo (1920-1969) was an accomplished sculptor and her mother, Sheojuk Toonoo (1928–) did some drawing in the 1960s. However, tuberculosis interrupted Ovilu's early childhood years, and she was sent by government health officials to hospitals in southern Canada on two different occasions—once to Clearwater Lake, Manitoba, for an entire year when she was five years old and again for more than two years to a hospital near Brandon, Manitoba, when she was seven and eight. The memories Ovilu Tunnillie holds from those formative years in the South remain in her mind and have inspired some of her recent carvings.

After regaining her health, Ovilu returned to the traditional camp life on Baffin Island. As a teenager in 1966, while living at the camp Igalallik, she was inspired to try her first soapstone carving by watching her father, Toonoo. At the time, Toonoo and others at Igalallik—including the noted artist, Niviaqsi, and Ovilu's grandmother, Kudjuakjuk—were carving regularly and taking their carvings to the new Co-op. In 1969, Ovilu moved to Cape Dorset with her parents and married Iola Tunnillie soon after.

Ovilu Tunnillie has been carving regularly since 1972, frequently experimenting with innovative subject matter and form in her well-crafted, inventive sculptures. Perhaps more pointedly than any other Cape Dorset artist, Ovilu Tunnillie uses the medium of sculpture both to convey the experiences of the traditional and changing Inuit culture and also to convey her own commentary on these experiences. She is an extremely accomplished and innovative sculptor and enjoys the process of creating art forms. During the 1970s, Ovilu also experimented with jewellery and cast bronze and worked for one year in 1978-79 as a printmaker in Cape Dorset's lithography studio.

Ovilu Tunnillie was featured in a solo exhibition, *Oviloo Toonoo*, at the Canadian Guild of Crafts Quebec in Montréal in 1981 and her sculptures have been included in several group exhibitions, including *Debut—Cape Dorset Jewellery*, Canadian Guild of Crafts Quebec (1976); *Arctic Vision: Art of the Canadian Inuit*, a travelling exhibition organized by the Department of Indian Affairs and Northern Development and Canadian Arctic Producers, Ottawa (1984-86); *Building on Strengths: New Inuit Art from the Collection*, Winnipeg Art Gallery (1988); and *Hermitage-89: New Exhibits*, Hermitage Museum, Leningrad, Soviet Union. Works by Ovilu Tunnillie are held in numerous public and private collections including the Canadian Guild of Crafts Quebec; the Canadian Museum of Civilization; the National Gallery of Canada; the Winnipeg Art Gallery; and the Hermitage Museum, Leningrad. The work by Ovilu Tunnillie that is held by the Hermitage Museum was a gift to the Soviet Union from Toronto collectors, Samuel and Esther Sarick.

Respected within her community for the strength of her artistic expression and for her leadership abilities, Ovilu Tunnillie was elected to the Board of Directors of the West Baffin Eskimo Co-operative in 1992. Increasingly, she is travelling to exhibition openings and assuming a new role of leadership in representing the artists of Cape Dorset.

Ovilu and her husband have five children and one grandchild living at home.

---

facing overleaf:
SHAMAN APPEARS
1970s
green stone
37 x 42 x 16 cm

unsigned
Collection of the
Images Art Gallery,
Toronto, Ontario

Some Thoughts
About My Life and Family

Ovilu Tunnillie

Ovilu Tunnillie with
adopted grand-
daughter, Tye, 1991

I AM PROUD of being able to do things on my own. My name is Ovilu Tunnillie. I was born on 20 December, 1949.

I will tell a story of my life experiences and about starting to do carvings. My first recollection is when I was two years old, being carried on my father's shoulders because my mother was carrying my younger brother in her *amauti*. Then in 1955, I was sent away to a hospital and did not return home until late fall of the following year on the ship *C.D. Howe*. Just a day after I returned home it snowed real hard. In those days, my parents did not live in Cape Dorset so I had to stay with other people until I could be taken by canoe to my parents' camp which was called Kangia. It was so cold travelling by canoe, especially after spending a year down South with my body not being accustomed to the cold any more.

I was so happy that I could spend that whole year with my parents. But in 1957 I was sent out again to another hospital in Montréal. I was heartbroken to have to leave my mother and father again. My father and I went to ask the nurses and government administrators not to send me away because I did not want to go. But we couldn't do anything, so I was sent to the hospital again by *C.D. Howe*, and I spent a lot of time crying under the table.

We arrived in Hamilton and I spent a month there, and then I was sent to a hospital in Ninga, Manitoba, near Brandon. At that place, I had an appointment to see two female nurses or doctors to be examined. I went, but I remember feeling so embarrassed because they took so long that I started wondering what was so different with my body. I was under their care for two years during 1957 and 1958. I really liked the dress and shoes I was given to wear. These two female nurses or doctors were in charge of the hospital, and I enjoyed my visits with them. I learned a lot about life while I was away as I was the only young girl there. I spent over two years there, and once I got used to it, I didn't mind it too much.

As I had my own room where I stayed, the room was filled with girl things that had been bought for me. I don't remember it being so much fun when another girl was brought in to where I was staying, and I did not like it at all when I was placed in a home for girls in 1959. I was placed at Bernadette Place where other girls were living, and I did not like it there because some girls were so immature, and there were girls who acted like they were little slaves to other girls there. I collected money in a jar that was given to me. But someone stole the money I had been saving, and whoever it was never did tell me. When I returned home, I did not bring all my belongings with me, and I have always regretted it.

Then during the springtime of that year, I think it was in April, I was sent back home to Cape Dorset by plane. And from there I was taken to my parents' camp by dog team. They were living at Nuvujuak at that time. While we travelled, I remember being so happy to be back home. I collected stones that I liked on the way. I had started collecting them in Ninga, especially the white stones. When I think back now, I went through some happy and some unhappy times.

After I had returned to my parents' camp, I had a hard time adjusting because apparently I had adopted too much of the southern culture and I had lost some of my Inuktitut. I watched my mother and aunt as we arrived, and they were crying because they were so happy to see me back, but I thought that this was what they did whenever someone came to their camp. Later on, I remember drawing pictures on pieces of paper that were given out at Cape Dorset, and my mother and aunt weren't too pleased. I thought that maybe they didn't want me back after all, and I regretted asking to be sent back home.

When someone brought in aged meat and I was offered some, I really thought that they were trying to kill me. I couldn't communicate with them in Inuktitut, and I did not like the taste! But later on, I realized that this kind of meat was a delicacy. I really craved milk. Since I did not like tea without milk in it, I thought my mother was just being eager for me to cry.

It was like I had just met my family for the first time. I couldn't understand their ways nor their language because I had gotten so used to the southern ways. I noticed that they could make things that seemed impossible to make—like the *qulliq*—and my father would go off hunting and bring back seal! Seal blubber would be used for oil in the lamp and used for cooking meals.

In July that year, we were to go to Cape Dorset. Because it was getting quite warm, I changed my clothing to underwear made out of cloth. My mother told me not to do that in full view because it just was not the thing to do. Inuit were brought up to be modest about their bodies, and the tent flaps had to be kept open then because it was so warm inside. The cultures of the Inuit and the *qallunaat* were very different then.

During 1959, my father, too, had to go away to a hospital. My father was sent to a hospital from Cape Dorset, and it was sad because he was the one who supplied us with food. I remember being afraid because we lived in our camp with other people, and one of them was not quite right in the head. I remember that we had to hide watches and knives when that person was allowed to go visiting. In 1960 when my father came back from down South, we moved to Igalallik.

Later on, after we had been back to our camp for a while, my mother gave birth and I thought that she'd come back to life when she was given cocoa to drink. It was a happy time when she gave birth even though we did not like nurses or doctors being around all the time. Later on, I would go along with my father by dog team. It was fun. Dogs were so useful then, pulling a sled with a number of people on it; they were our only means of travel in those days.

Then in 1966 when I was seventeen, I made my first

carving to see if I had a talent for it like my father did, and I was so happy to get things I wanted when I got paid for it. I bought canvas and duffle with the money. I found, too, that I enjoyed making carvings. Along with my father, other people were carving at Igalallik—Niviaqsi and my grandmother, Kudjuakjuk. And later on, living with my mother, I started doing things and making things that she did. I had always wanted to make a toy tent. My father bought me the material to make that and some other things so I could make things. I then made a real tent and a parka with an outer shell.

My father died in 1969, shot with a rifle. I got married then, even though I still felt too young, and I had my first child then. After my daughter was born, we would live out on the land to hunt and would go to get soapstone by canoe.

In 1970, I spent six months in Cape Dorset. In 1972 when my daughter, Alashua, was born, I started making carvings again. We have been here in Cape Dorset since then. The way I carve has changed along with the ways of life now. I used to make carvings with only an axe and a file, but now I use other tools like the electric ones because of my asthma. At times it was difficult to complete my carvings because I had six children to bring up and there were always household chores to do. I have had seven children, but one of them died. Even though it has been rough at times, I do not regret any of it.

I have always tried to make a living by carving, even though carving isn't the same as other people's jobs now. I have been carving ever since my daughter was born in 1972. Sometimes it gets difficult to envision what the carving will be and what the options are. Remembering what I have made, I always wish I had done more, but that is okay.

I can make carvings like a man can, and I enjoy it because my father taught me. We would travel by dog team during the month of May, and as soon as I was untied from the sled, I would go to look at rocks and collect them. I have always been fascinated by rocks for as long as I can remember, probably because I would make things out of soapstone later in my life. Soapstone was always used by the Inuit for many other things as well, like *qulliq* and pots. Men are accustomed to being outside carving or hunting. Because of being a female, I was meant to be indoors, so I had a hard time getting accustomed to doing my carvings outdoors, especially during the eight months when we have snow. We only have warm weather for four months of the year. I encourage the other women to make carvings outdoors as well, because it shows that women are strong too in their own way.

I am happy to have been given a chance to tell my story about being a woman carver and my experiences in life.

MAN AND BEAR
1974–76
bronze, 1/1 (edition: 1)
4.9 x 3.8 x 2.3 cm
unsigned
Collection of the
Canadian Guild of
Crafts Quebec,
Montréal, Quebec
426

Only a few pieces in
this style were created
between 1971 and 1976
in Cape Dorset.
Limited runs of bronze
cast in the lost-wax
process were created in
the course of experi-
ments carried out by
the artist.

DOGS FIGHTING
circa 1975
(Original title: *Caribou
Attacked by Wolves.*
Changed by artist.)
green stone
43.3 x 38.9 x 4 cm
unsigned
Gift of M.F. Feheley,
Toronto, Ontario, 1985
National Gallery
of Canada, Ottawa
29284

*I have always liked
dogs and for a little
while I carved dogs....
I have carved this
depicting dogs in a
fight. Dogs used to get
into a fight with each
other.*
1991 interview with Odette
Leroux

COMPOSITION
OF OWLS
circa 1977
green stone
23.5 x 13.5 x 74.5 cm
signed
Private Collection,
Waterloo, Ontario

*I have tried to carve
different things (sub-
jects) and I had heard
that carvings of owls
are well liked. I tried to
make it look good and
interesting, but as I see
it—it doesn't look that
beautiful but it is interesting.*
1991 interview with Odette
Leroux

OWL
circa 1979
green stone
29 x 31.5 x 5 cm
unsigned
Gift of M.F. Feheley,
Toronto, Ontario, 1985
National Gallery of
Canada, Ottawa
29309

THOUGHT
CREATES MEANING
circa 1980
green stone
41 x 35 x 15 cm
unsigned
IV-C-5490

The hand represents the grip of drink on Inuit. I thought about the drinks taking grip on Inuit. ... This [the head] is the mind. Inuit were given alcohol by the government. The hand, which is a symbol of Inuit, is pointing a finger at the government official.

No one in particular, but qallunaat (white people). You will notice the man isn't wearing kamiit because the person's white. If I'd meant to depict Inuit as if they had brought it (alcohol), then it would feature an Inuk. I am attempting to depict that the man is

thinking; I'm attempting to depict that his mind is being affected by this head. This was my thought at the time. I disliked alcohol for what it can do to people.
1991 interview with Odette Leroux and 1992 interview with Marion E. Jackson and Odette Leroux

This is a work of aesthetic inspiration and not intended as a social commentary.
Statement by artist.

FOOTBALL PLAYER
1981
green stone
52 x 29 x 17 cm
signed
Gift of the Department
of Indian Affairs and
Northern
Development, 1989
Inuit Cultural Institute,
Rankin Inlet,
Northwest Territories
1.81.21

This is the depiction of a white man because it's not wearing a parka.... [The story about this sculpture is] about the fact that I can now watch [the football game].... I try to think about the end result of the carving as to where it will go.
1991 interview with Odette Leroux

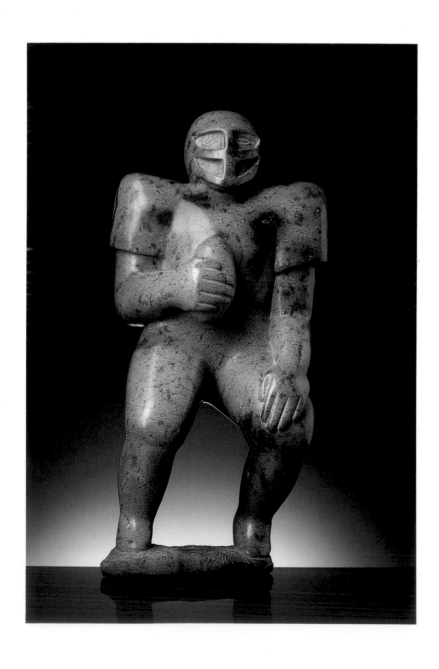

SEAMAN, SEAWOMAN
AND FISH
circa 1981
green stone
12.5 x 50.3 x 6.3 cm
signed
Gift of Dr. Dorothy M.
Stillwell, 1986
National Gallery of
Canada, Ottawa
29448

I have only heard about mermaids or human marine beings. I cannot say that they exist nor can I say they do not exist since I have never seen one myself…. This is a taleelayu [sea goddess]. They are marine beings and fish are also marine beings. Since they are both marine beings, I just included the fish to go with the mermaids…. Those mermaids are sea inhabitors and one time I used to make a lot of them. I thought, 'Did they have a lifestyle like the Inuit?' It was entirely out of my personal imagination that I did it…. But I like carving the mermaids.

1991 interview with Odette Leroux

*My favourite work is
on taleelayu, women
figures. I don't know, I
think they can be
either one (man or
woman).... I did it
only from my imagina-
tion.... I cannot tell
the stories of them.*
1992 interview with Marion E.
Jackson and Odette Leroux

HAWK TAKING OFF
circa 1987
green stone
17.4 x 72 x 38 cm
signed
IV-C-5488

With my carvings, right now the bird is my favourite subject to carve. The things that are simple in detail, that is with my own thinking, and I create them out of my own imagination.... Right now, I like carving birds with wings spread out. I like to *carve the stone very thin on the wings. When I do this, a lot of the stone comes off because I try to take the bulk of the weight off.*
1991 interview with Odette Leroux

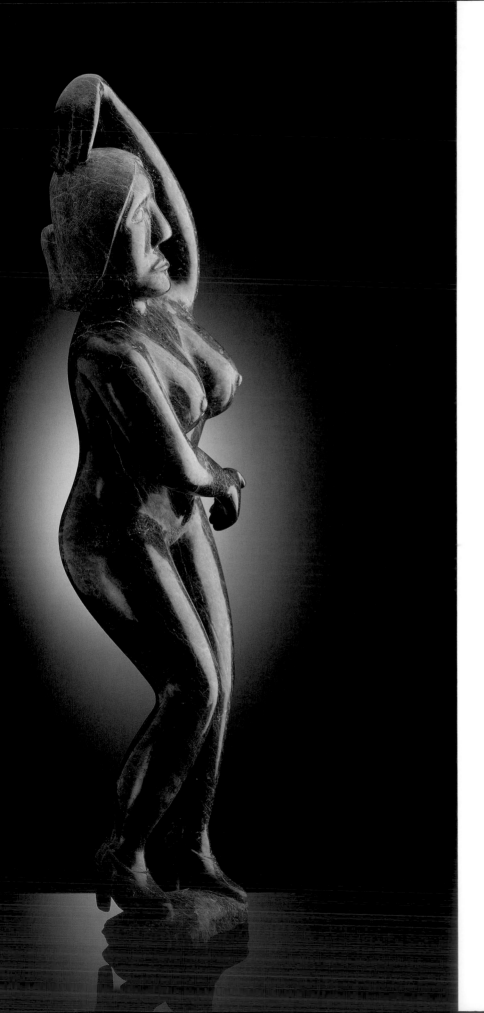

WOMAN
ON HIGH HEELS
1987
dark green stone
67 x 20.5 x 15 cm
unsigned
IV-C-5489

I usually do also some [subject matters] that [are] peculiar to me that I have seen before, that I don't see every day. And this is a true white woman, that is why she is wearing high heeled shoes.
1992 interview with Marion E. Jackson and Odette Leroux

Inuit women hardly ever wear high-heeled shoes.... I was in Montreal sometimes in the 1970s. While there, I used to watch T.V. and saw nude women with high heels. They show those on T.V.... I like the end result very much of that piece.
1991 interview with Odette Leroux

WOMAN PASSED OUT
1987
green stone
48 x 28 x 25 cm
unsigned
IV-C-5501

The liquor was brought up from the white people, not from Inuit. This one is taking a drink. This is a drunken person that tempted the others to drink more. This person is passed out, because the alcohol can make you do anything, like this one. A woman doesn't mean to be the way she is here, but although she may never be one to be seen in as such, but it happens after she had too much to drink.
1992 interview with Marion E. Jackson and Odette Leroux

This is a work of aesthetic inspiration and not intended as a social commentary.
Statement by artist.

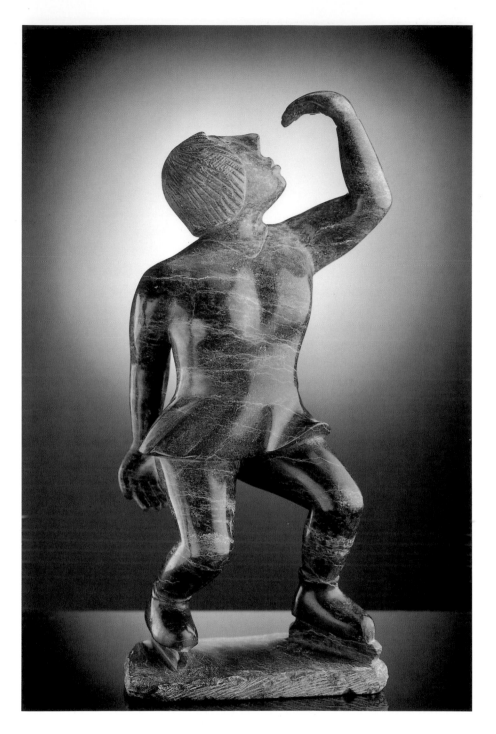

SKATER
1988
green stone
48.5 x 23 x 15.5 cm
signed
IV-C-5500

She is in a competition.
1992 interview with Marion E.
Jackson and Odette Leroux

HAWK LANDED
circa 1989
dark green stone
12 x 34.5 x 29.2 cm
signed
IV-C-5487

The wings and the beak and the feet are ones I like to do because the end result ... I try to carve a bird that has a flow to it in looking at it.... I liked doing my bird. I find a great joy when the stone starts to take a shape.
1991 interview with Odette Leroux

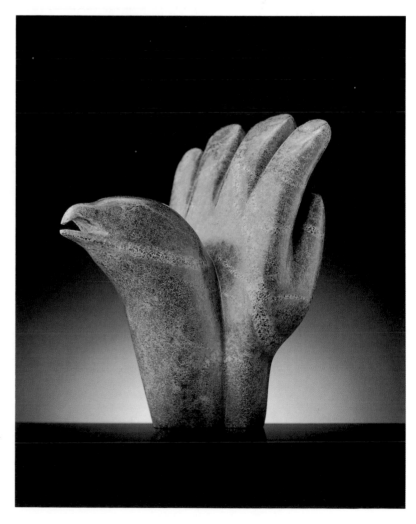

I MADE THIS
WITH MY HANDS
1990
green stone
19.1 x 11.5 x 17.5 cm
signed
Gift of Carrie Beth and
Lani Jill Seidelman,
Toronto, Ontario, 1992
IV-C-5492

A hand is capable of carving a gyrfalcon.... I Made This with My Hands.... I made this while I was thinking that the hands can be extremely creative. The hands are the most useful part of us.
1992 interview with Marion E. Jackson and Odette Leroux

MY MOTHER
AND MYSELF
1990
dark green stone
23.3 x 20.5 x 9.8 cm
signed
IV-C-5486

Syllabic inscription on
the front of the sculp-
ture: *Ovilu Tunnillie,
Kinngait [Cape Dorset]*

*These are also telling
stories of my mother,
myself and my brother,
Jutai. It tells about
when I first got back
with my parents. That
was in 1959 when I got
back home. She had a
baby... I actually saw
her giving birth, that
was my first experience
to see a baby coming*

*out of a mother. I used
to have band hair in
front when I was a lit-
tle girl.* My Mother and
Myself—*that was
when my father was
away down South. I
meant to put my older
brother, he was there
too, but I wanted only
to explain about
myself. The one she is*

*carrying in her back is
Jutai Toonoo, the one I
watched at his birth.*
1992 interview with Marion E.
Jackson and Odette Leroux

THIS HAS TOUCHED MY LIFE
1991–92
dark green stone
woman: 42.5 x 23.5 x 18 cm
woman and child: 42 x 48.5 x 26.5 cm
man: 47 x 22.5 x 13.5 cm
car: 7.5 x 23.5 x 11.4 cm
signed
IV-C-5498 a-d

When I was in a hospital away from home, it was during the years of 1957, 1958 and 1959. While I was away, I was taken by automobile to see these two women from the hospital where I stayed. A woman and a man who were social workers accompanied me

on this trip, to where, I don't know. Maybe it was during the month of August.

When I saw these two, I really noticed the way they were dressed and their faces were hidden. Well, I could see them but they were unrecognizable as they

wore hats that had lace pulled down in front of their faces and they each had purses. I really looked at how they were dressed and having seen them like this has been the most memorable for me. I have not met any white person such as these two yet. I wonder

sometimes if they were ashamed of their faces because I've never seen that before.... The hospital where I stayed was in Ninga, somewhere in Manitoba. [It] was after we moved out of the hospital that we went to see these two veiled women. So this has been the

most memorable part of my life while I was away there. And I returned to Cape Dorset in the month of May.

Written by Ovilu Tunnillie in February 1992 with additional material from interviews with Marion E. Jackson and Odette Leroux.

Good Memories

Ann Meekitjuk Hanson

MY EARLIEST MEMORIES of carvings are of Annowal-koolook and his miniature ivory caribou. I remember them because they were so tiny in his big hands. He held each tiny white marvel at eye level, dwarfing it between his thumb and index finger. He was sitting on a box by his wife's corner in the hut. His wife was sewing while her *qulliq* evenly flickered flames underneath the cooking pot hanging over it. There were no sounds except for gentle rasping from the ivory and the file, Pitseolak's needle and thread penetrating through her unfinished garment rhythmically, and faint gurgling of bursting bubbles in the cooking pot emitting the aroma of *uujuq*. This fond memory is embedded in me for three reasons: survival, social order and art.

I was born at Qakuqtute, a camp near Lake Harbour which my mother and father occupied every year while they waited for the sea ice to break up. It was their spring camp. My father, Meekitjuk, following his ancestors' survival instincts, moved from camp to camp according to seasons and provided for his family and the people. I have no memories of my father because he died when I was four years old. I am told by my uncles that he was a good provider, kind, generous and caring. These qualities enabled him to be the leader of his people until his death.

I was born in May 1946, towards the end of the nomadic way of life for the Inuit. I feel fortunate to have experienced what I call "the real Inuk way of life." At that time, my father was still very independent, completely living by animals of the land and sea and relying for survival on himself and his fellow Inuit for their abilities and ingenuity. They did this by hunting the animals and following the natural laws and social order set by generations of humans who strived for a better and more comfortable life.

The natural laws I am talking about are just that: laws set by nature and followed by the people who must live by them in order to survive, to conserve, to pass on life. One such law is the weather. My father had to know and obey the weather so his family would not starve. He became an expert forecaster by knowing the shape of the clouds, the speed of the winds, the colour of the sky, the smell in the air or the colour of the moon. He carefully observed the ice conditions, the swells of the sea, the tides, the inlets, land points, snow conditions, the currents of the rivers and lakes. He learned all the animals' migration routes, their habits, their food chains, their gestations, their strengths and weaknesses. Most of all, to the best of his understanding, he learned his own place on this earth where he shared oneness in a space meant for harmony.

The social order was another aspect of basic survival when my father lived. I am told my father was a peaceful man. He was not bossy or domineering in his style of leadership. When he had to make a decision, he made it to suit the lifestyle of the people in their time. Most of the decisions had to do with making sure the people had comfortable lives free of starvation and animosity. When a family wished to move to another location in pursuit of plenty, my father gave consent with full blessing but he had to make sure that it was what the people wanted. This meant that people had to be near enough to reach other people for help if or when there was starvation but, at the same time, free of depending on others all the time. In my father's time, this was called "independence at arm's length" without freeloading on others and yet being able to accept others' generosity without shame. Social order was knowing each other's need. My mother knew how to deliver her neighbour's baby, to care for the dying and the sick, to counsel the depressed, to teach the naive, and to seek innovative ways to make life easier by creating new garments or tools. This process of creation to make life easier leads to the arts.

When I was growing up, I had no understanding of art because I have never been able to set a special category for art.

My only understanding of art is this: art is life. With art, our life is shaped by looking for ways to make living easier. In the beginning of my story, I talked about Annowalkoolook and his ivory. At another time, I remember Annowalkoolook making a clasp for his wife's *amauti* so she wouldn't have a hard time tying her sash around the waist. The clasp was ivory, oval shaped, smaller than an egg. There was a hole at the end to tie the end of the sash. There was a hook at the other end. It was flat on the bottom and rounded on the top. On the top, Annowalkoolook made it beautiful by designing ornate drawings on it. It was so beautiful to look at and yet its purpose was to simplify the tying of bulky knots on his wife's *amauti*.

Through the years that I worked with Canadian Broadcasting Corporation (CBC), I have been fortunate to talk with many modern Inuit artists, people who make carvings, prints, drawings as well as singers, dancers and storytellers. It is one job I thoroughly enjoy because I get close to people who create things to make life easier for themselves. Of course, today artists create things for extra money so they can provide better for their families and themselves. I remember so many wonderful creators. I will single out three women. First, allow me to express my great admiration for all the artists living today. When I see creations of animals, landscapes, legends on stone, figures, mother and child on stone, I am awed and greatly inspired by such creativity and am mildly envious of the artists' wonderful gift.

I remember Elisapee. She was the wife of Noah Piugatuq in Igloolik. I was in Igloolik around 1978 collecting stories for our CBC Inuktitut program, *Tausunni*. I visited Noah and Elisapee because someone told me that they would be good to tell stories and sing songs and that they knew so much about Inuit history. After explaining the purpose of my visit and offering a proper introduction in the Inuit way (telling them of my ancestral history), we had tea. Elisapee took me to the room where she had been carving. She led me to a small table which had a igloo carving on it. She reached for the upper half of the snow house, lifted it and there they were! We laughed! I was speechless. I was absolutely awed and amazed. Inside the snow house were people, dogs, children, babies and the necessities for living. Elisapee had created in stone a grandmother telling a legend to her family. The whole family was listening to the legend while the dogs were by the door protecting the family. Elisapee told the story while explaining what was in the snow house piece by piece. She sang the song of her story in stone while moving each person. I recorded her story while she talked about her carving. In her modesty, she would laugh at her own work while I listened. She had a wonderful deep husky voice that is quite unforgettable. When Elisapee finished her story, she gave me an ivory comb, which, she said, was given to her by an elder many, many years ago. She wanted to give the comb because she enjoyed the stories, legends, songs and life histories of the Inuit on the radio. Then she offered to walk me home because she did not want me to be afraid of the dogs. After being with Elisapee and Noah, I was greatly inspired to continue to do cultural programs and to pass on stories as they did.

Pitseolak Ashoona of Cape Dorset was one of my relatives. She passed on a different form of art through her drawings. Pitseolak drew a picture for me which not only hangs on the wall, but in my heart as well. I was translating Pitseolak's book *Pictures out of My Life* with Dorothy Eber in the early 1970s while I was expecting our fourth daughter, Udluriak. Pitseolak wanted to show me how she had babies before doctors and nurses. Through her art, Pitseolak drew three women delivering a baby the way she remembered it, in vivid colours, representing a happy time. She, too, laughed about her drawing, saying that she could not get everything "right." When she did that drawing for me, it inspired me to do a program on how we Inuit women had babies with midwives and how names were picked for the newborns. In the 1970s, we had begun to pick English or foreign names for our babies. I wanted to encourage our women to pick Inuit names for our newborns to pass on tradition. Thus, Udluriak Ooa was named after my aunt Udluriak and my great-aunt Ooa. By her subtle suggestion through her art, Pitseolak passed on a very important tradition.

Leetia Panipakooshook of Pond Inlet was one of the most inspiring storytellers I have ever known. I first met her in 1977. Again, I was collecting stories for our radio program for the CBC. She was a small woman with a soft, friendly voice that was so soothing. I was uncomfortable because she was blind. She felt my apprehension and made me feel at ease by talking to me. Leetia had so many stories that it is hard to pick one to talk about. I will talk about the one that remains in me the most.

We were sitting on the cool floor. It was early in the day. The room was bare. There was hardly any furniture except for some chairs and a table. There were curtains on the windows. The room sounded hollow. Leetia was facing me as I held the microphone. Without my asking questions, Leetia started her story. The story was about shamanism.

Leetia said she was a little girl when people still practised shamanism behind the clergyman's back. They hid their rituals because the new belief discouraged shamanism. She talked about their great chanting, a special song that only shamans could sing. She did not want to imitate the chants because of her new belief. She said some of the rituals were so overpoweringly scary. Sometimes I could hardly hear her because her voice would trail off. Sometimes I could not understand because she used the old Inuktitut. I did not want to interrupt her too often for fear of breaking her train of thought. Besides, it is considered rude to interrupt an elder while she is talking. She described one shaman who was able to change the appearance of his face. She imitated how he did it. She put her hand entirely over her face, slid it down slowly, and then the face would be completely changed. Leetia said people decided to get rid of shamanism because it was too difficult. She said it was hard work to continue.

Leetia was a wonderful seamstress and a musician in addition to being a storyteller. She made parkas, duffle socks, slippers, and *kamiit*. She gave me one of the parkas she made. Leetia played squeeze box music. She played the Scottish and Irish tunes and named what kind of dances they were suited for. When she played, the room was filled with music. When she finished, I just kissed her because I did not know what else to do. Leetia's art lives in many people today through her stories and songs.

I marvel at people who have the ability to create and to stir us up during the sad times or happy times through their art. Whether through storytelling, carvings, songs, prints, music or writing, it is art that shapes our life to make it bearable, joyful, memorable, profitable or just plain worth living.

Also, while art has enriched many people monetarily, it also enhances our language. Through carvings, some of the old Inuktitut terms have stayed alive. Some examples include *Lumajuuq*. This is a legend about a cruel mother who became half whale, half woman; she is a favourite subject with many carvers from different parts of the North. Another example is *natturaq*, the ivory clasp used to minimize the bulky tie knots in an *amauti*. *Tusarautiniq* is a term referring to how we speak to each other using terms indicating how we are related. This was illustrated by Pitscolak when she drew that picture of three women assisting in a birth. Of course, the names of all the animals; fish, birds, plants, flowers, landscapes and the sea are all documented in the art.

This is the story of my involvement in the arts with my people. I live among the artists, and it is a wonderful feeling… tinged with envy and awe.

Ann Meekitjuk Hanson
1946–

Born in the mid-1940s at Qakuqtute, a small camp near Lake Harbour, Ann Meekitjuk Hanson spent her early childhood following the traditional Inuit lifestyle. She lived with aunts, uncles and various relatives until she went to school in Iqaluit in 1958. Later moving to Toronto where she lived with foster parents, Murray and Kay Cotterill, Ann completed her schooling in English and received secretarial training. In 1965, she became a broadcaster for the Canadian Broadcasting Corporation. In addition to covering current affairs, public interest stories, humour and lifestyles, Ann Hanson, with fellow broadcasters, successfully initiated Inuktitut cultural programming on the CBC in an effort to preserve the Inuktitut language and culture.

In 1987, Hanson returned to school to take a two-year journalism course at Arctic College in Iqaluit. She graduated in 1989 and currently does freelance broadcasting for radio and television. Her excellent language skills and familiarity with both traditional Inuit culture and the culture of southern Canada in addition to her warm and outgoing personality enable her to nourish understanding and respect for the Inuit culture and to facilitate communication between cultures. Recognized as a leader in the North, Ann Meekitjuk Hanson served as Deputy Commissioner of the Northwest Territories for four years. She and her husband, Bob Hanson, live in Iqaluit and have five grown daughters and accumulating grandchildren.

My Career Experiences

Annie Manning

MY NAME is Annie Manning. I would like to talk first about being Justice of the Peace. When I completed my teacher education in 1976, I came back to Cape Dorset to teach.

During the spring of 1978, I was asked if I would be interested in becoming a Justice of the Peace. I was told that an Inuk woman was needed to serve as a Justice of the Peace. Because I had so many other commitments that came with being a teacher, I wasn't sure that I wanted the job. But when I thought about how many break the law in our community and how it might be better to have an Inuk as a Justice of the Peace, I ended up taking on the job. I also took the job because it seemed useful when I looked to the future of Inuit women. Since it is not only males who can do the job, I thought it was about time for us to stand up as women to show that we are capable. I was the first female Inuk on Baffin Island to become a Justice of the Peace.

I served as Justice of the Peace in Cape Dorset for five or six years until my licence ended. Serving as a Justice of the Peace helped me see things in a different light in our community and not only things that concerned me as a teacher. Because I was a Justice of the Peace and a woman, there were times when it was hard to deal with things. However, it is important for people who break the law to know that not only the *qallunaat* are able to manage that kind of job: Inuit women can also do the job.

I also learned a lot about the law by performing and reading up on it and attending courses on being a Justice of the Peace. Before I attended the course on law, it was not too good for me because I had no knowledge at all on the subject. I had to start out only by reading and practice. Later on, a number of us Inuit who were Justices of the Peace across the Northwest Territories and one Indian woman from the Western Arctic region were sent to Yellowknife to attend a course. The Indian woman and I were the only women in the group. Others also said that when they were asked to serve as a Justice of the Peace in their area they did not have too much knowledge of law, but that they agreed to take on the job when they thought about the future.

I would also like to talk a bit about being a teacher at the school. In 1971, I first became a teacher's assistant at Lake Harbour. Then the next year, I returned to Cape Dorset and was assistant at our school here for two years. After that, I was asked if I would like to become a qualified teacher, and I agreed because I enjoyed teaching. Teachers' assistants then were sent to Fort Smith and Iqaluit and sometimes Saskatoon to take teachers' training. I really enjoy being a teacher because I enjoy dealing with children.

We have to think about the future of our students, and they too have to become aware that Inuit have the capability to do all kinds of jobs. Also, we Inuit have to teach our children the traditional way of life and encourage them to make something of themselves—starting when they are just beginning school and continuing on so they can get employment confidently when they graduate. If children are made aware that they can have pride in themselves and pride in being Inuit, there is no limit to what they can make of themselves.

The education system has improved quite a lot through the use of theme planning around subjects related to our land. For example, during the early fall, ships come in with supplies; we can use everything that is related to ships to teach the students. Also, students really enjoy subjects related to fish, polar bears and other animals because these subjects are things that they know about and that are related to their future. Now, because spring has arrived and the ducks are again coming back, I direct my teaching towards spring and towards birds. We have seasonal animals here, so the seasons are helpful for teaching about how certain animals were hunted and caught in the old days before there were any rifles. We can learn more of what life used to be like for the Inuit and how it is today.

What we teach now is going to be very useful in the future. Specialists have thought of ways to stop the drop-out rate and have suggested that if students are taught about subjects that concern them in their lives, the drop-out rate could be reduced. That makes sense for our future. For example, the animals connect us as Inuit from traditional times to the present and we teach how the animals were hunted then and now. These things are connected to our future.

When I was going to school, the first things that were taught to us then by the *qallunaat* were about trees, and our readers were *Dick and Jane*. What we could have been taught was lost in the beginning because the school curriculum was not too well prepared. The new theme planning for curriculum will become very useful for our future, and the government and other officials are now more interested to see what we can do. If we teach what is useful to our lives and environment, we are more capable of standing on our own.

I also feel that artists are very useful to us. They show us that they, too, can hold jobs—drawing and carving and telling stories about our traditional ways of life and about the modern ways. They also show us that women, too, have the ability to do these things. I say that because women have a lot to share and are less shy to speak up than men are. Women have to take leadership in drawing and telling stories because when children see and hear these things, they become more aware and they learn what life was like for the Inuit. Talented artists who can do drawings and carvings can show our children what life was like, and those things can be useful in their future and in helping our children to make something of themselves.

My mother's father, Peter Pitseolak, was a leader at Keatuk and also here at Cape Dorset in the early days. From what I was told, he was approached by the *qallunaat* when they first started coming up north and asked if it would be a good idea to set up a school at Cape Dorset. When he agreed to that, the school was built here. The school was one of the things that helped me later on when I decided I wanted to become a teacher. It seemed that wanting to become a teacher had been directed into my thinking.

My father worked for a living at the Hudson's Bay Company store ever since I was quite small, and we lived at Cape Dorset year-round. His working for a living had an influence on my wanting to work for a living, too. I started to think that I, too, can stand on my own two feet by working for a living. And that is the only way we can live now—by making an income. We can advance ourselves by showing our capabilities.

I also would like to talk about the time my grandparents lived at Keatuk and we would be taken there by dog team during the wintertime. I used to really enjoy going there by dog team because it was so seldom we would travel by dog team then. I enjoyed the different games that my grandfather would have us do while we visited—racing and other games, plus using the pencils and erasers he had saved for us. I also remember that during the summertime, we would go collecting berries. My older sister, Ainiaq would always take us; we would go across the *kiputiit* to collect berries and try to fill our tea kettles. I remember thinking to myself that when I grew bigger I would be able to fill one of those tea kettles with berries, because in those days I could fill only one of those smaller containers. But as it turns out, I still have not been able to fill a tea kettle!

I would also like to talk about the different things that arrive here now. As a woman, I know that we like to have clothes washers. Other Inuit women before us used to wash clothing only by hand. Sometimes their skin would become raw, so I really do appreciate having a washer and dryer, even though we can still use a clothes line if we want to. Having a washer and dryer is very useful, especially in the wintertime. We also appreciate having couches and chairs.

I have also thought about wanting to own things right away soon as we see them. Perhaps, through education, we could learn to want things but not have to get them right away. I feel that we have to learn to save money we make for future use, rather than using up the money as soon as we get it. I feel that Inuit need education on how to save the money they earn, to spend their earnings wisely and to have emergency money handy in case something should happen or a relative might need help later on. I have thought about the fact that we need to save our money at banks, and the fact that when one of us does come up with a large amount of money, we need not spend it all right away.

I also would like women to learn and become more aware of the law. Today some women get assaulted physically by their husbands or boyfriends, and that is not the way it is supposed to be. Many women—especially Inuit women—do not speak up if they are being abused. Some do speak up right away, but more are too afraid to speak up about the abuse they are getting and feel they cannot press charges. I feel that automatic charges should be put in effect for special assault cases in the near future. It is about time that our capabilities as women are shown and that we are not drowned out by these things. Ever since I became a Justice of the Peace, I have wanted to see spouses treat each other with the respect that they should have for each other. That is the only way it should work—that we never belittle our spouse; that we make them presentable to others; that we not mistreat them but that we encourage them to be all that they can be. Otherwise, all that might have been possible will just get lost. That is the way it has been for some women who could have done more but have given up because of the abuse they have received.

Before we got to know more *qallunaat* in our community,

we were not too aware of some things. We didn't know too much about such things as fruits. I remember one time when I was young and we were asked to go to the nursing station for tea. My cousin and I went over with some other girls. What I remember most about that occasion is those plastic grapes. I took some, thinking they were real, and when I learned they weren't, I threw them out in the street. I found out later that my cousin knew I took them. Even today when I see grapes I remember that time!

New things for sale are always coming up. I remember when we got our new wringer washer, and my mother told me not to touch it because I was still too young. But I decided to try to wash clothes anyway when my parents went fishing and I was babysitting. I put such a large load in the washer that the machine started to smoke. Then when I was wringing the clothes out, my hand and arm went through the wringer with the clothes until we stopped the machine. We can be so dumb about things that are new to us. I was so afraid of getting in trouble that I have never yet told my mother about the time the washing machine started smoking.

I always enjoy the summer season when the weather is warm and we can dry our clothing outdoors and go out to the land to cook. I always remember when I was young, camping out in a tent even though we had our house and visiting other people who were also camping out. One time our tent came undone from severe winds, and the only thing I thought to save was my jacket that had been given to me by the Hudson's Bay Company boss! I enjoy summer seasons most because more animals come around then, and my brothers have always supplied me with wildlife food and other things. Also, I have become aware that people smile more, maybe because it is not as cold or maybe because they are just happier.

Annie Manning
1952–

Annie Manning was born in Cape Dorset in 1952 at the time the small community was beginning to form around the Hudson's Bay Company and the old Baffin Trading Company posts. Her father, Tommy Manning, worked for the Hudson's Bay Company, and her mother, Udluriak, was the daughter of the great South Baffin camp leader, Peter Pitseolak. As a child, Annie frequently travelled to her grandfather's camp at Keatuk, though her childhood years were spent primarily in the close vicinity of Cape Dorset. Annie was one of the first to attend school in Cape Dorset in the 1950s, and she developed very early the language skills and thirst for knowledge that would lead her to a career in teaching and to a position of leadership in her community.

Throughout her life, Annie has enjoyed the dependable support of her large and influential family, and she also cites Brian Lewis, one of the early Cape Dorset teachers, as instrumental in helping her think about the possibilities for her future. Upon completing her own education, Annie moved to Lake Harbour in 1971 to become a classroom assistant and later undertook the same role in Cape Dorset. Since completing a year of Teacher Training in Fort Smith in 1975-1976, Annie has been a fully certified classroom teacher in both Cape Dorset and Spence Bay and, from 1979 to 1984, she also served as the first woman Justice of the Peace in Cape Dorset. She is a recognized leader in her community and takes her responsibility as a teacher and as an active member of her community very seriously.

While not viewing herself as an artist, Annie Manning is an accomplished seamstress who makes dolls in traditional Inuit clothing. She is the mother of three sons.

Traditional and Contemporary Roles of Inuit Women

Minnie Aodla Freeman

AS A MODERN Inuit woman, I would like to know if men and women were equal partners when the rules for women were adopted in the Inuit culture. I know such wondering will never be answered satisfactorily as I was born too late. The rules that Inuit women live by have been practised for 4,000 years, and in many areas of the Arctic they are still very much in use.

In the first place, all the rules and cultural values are transmitted both verbally and spiritually at the time of a child's birth. At that time, six people are present. All are there to make sure that the rules will be followed and then passed on and used by the new parents.

Traditionally, training begins at the earliest age possible, depending on both the psychological and mental development of the child. One of the six people present at the birth monitors the child's rate of development which the Inuit believe varies from child to child. Age, in number of years, has never been important to Inuit people; they have always watched the psychological and mental aptitudes of children or other people. The monitor does not guide the child directly. He or she has to discuss the needs of the child with the parents. Parents and grandparents and whoever has direct responsibility for the child practise the monitor's directives.

Though initially both boys and girls are brought up to follow the same household rules, after a time the expected chores begin to change. Boys help their fathers and learn all about hunting and providing for the household's food and material needs. Girls, on the other hand, remain at home and learn from their mothers. Even what they eat or what parts of the animals they eat changes. For instance, girls are taught to eat the heads of any animals so that their fathers, brothers, or whatever man they ate the head for will be a good shot, never missing the animal's head. Although women do get other parts of the animals to eat, the head is always on her side of the plate.

Traditionally, Inuit families eat out of one dish with each part placed for each person in a certain part of the plate or stone dish. As a stranger, if you get part of the dish, there is no doubt that you are very welcome in the family. Otherwise, you will get your own plate.

One of the important lessons girls learned very quickly was, and still is today, about other children. Girls babysit from an early age while their mothers handle other important household responsibilities such as preparing skins for various purposes. In the traditional times, a girl would also chew skins in order to soften them for her mother's use, and in the winter, girls brought in clean snow to cover the floor of the igloo. Of course, it is the responsibility of one of the original six birth attendants to ensure that the girl is being well taught by her mother.

All the rules were established before the girl's birth. The six people chosen at her birth remain involved in her life as long as they live. They always have to be a good example to the child. They give the child what they have made especially for him or her. For instance, a child might receive a little *ulu*, or a new *amauti*, or whatever pertains to bringing a girl into womanhood.

The six people are responsible for ensuring that the appropriate rules and values are followed. The cycle is repeated when the girl eventually becomes a woman. Inuit consider that a girl becomes a woman when she gets her first menstruation. Then the rules the young woman has to follow became very heavy. Inuit believe that one cannot control natural sexual desires at a young age. The young woman is kept ever so busy so that she will never have time to become promiscuous. That is why there were no unwanted pregnancies during traditional Inuit times. All that has now changed because a lot of rules for young women have died out.

One of the six people involved at her birth is a boy she will eventually marry when she becomes a woman. That is another reason why Inuit did not have unwanted babies in traditional times. Today, the contemporary Inuit girl is quite free. She goes to school away from home. She has a job away from home. She even tries to choose her own husband away from home.

The child who is most admired is usually kind, sweet-natured, thoughtful and has a sense of fear. He or she will always be trusted. As a girl grows, even her personality is subjected to monitoring, correction and approval. One of the important qualities required of a woman is the ability to be patient and to work without ever complaining. This is a quality important not just within the family, but to maintain wider harmony in the sometimes-demanding Arctic environment. When she marries, her husband is taught not to take advantage of her patience. The expression is "not to own a dog." He is also subject to monitoring by his own monitor.

Most of the traditional values have been carried over to modern Inuit women today. In fact, some cannot be abandoned if one is to become an Inuk woman. The rules do not change a great deal. The mother still attends to all her chores, and the six birth attendants are still required at home births. Traditionally, six people have always been involved during the birth of a child; two of these, the predictor and the midwife, always attended, whereas the other four may or may not be present during the birth. But today when a woman has to give birth, she sometimes has to go to the hospital in the community or to a hospital in the South. Then the predictor and the midwife are not able to attend. Still, they continue to be very carefully chosen by grandparents and parents. And the ceremonies are practised when the mother and child are back home from the hospital. All the rules and cultural values are transmitted both verbally and spiritually at that time.

Some of the very strong rules and values one is brought up

with just never leave, no matter how much one has learned about other outside cultural values. For instance, Inuit women have experienced great changes over the last fifty years but are still able to smile at any time to anyone. Most of them were not born to the electrical or mechanical world, yet they have adapted very successfully to electric stoves and ovens, washing machines and dryers, irons, kettles and hair dryers, not to mention electric blankets.

Even though they are in the midst of this electrical world, the women have not discarded their own women's corners. Each Inuk woman has always had her own corner in an igloo or *qarmaq* . Traditionally, she conducted all her duties from that corner. She had her seal-oil lamp, half-moon knife, sewing needles, loon-skin bag, and all her treasured knick-knacks. Where does one find this corner in a four-bedroom house today? If visiting an Inuit home in the contemporary world of the Arctic, one finds there is always a woman's corner in the living room. However, if there happen to be two or three women in the household, then each has her own corner in her own bedroom. In that corner she keeps her sewing needles, her favourite treasured items and knick-knacks.

Another quality that has not been obscured, and hopefully will never be lost, is the smile of Inuit women. Inuit watch closely for smiles, and there are many different kinds of smiles. If you have been taught well by one of the monitors how to read them, the smiles have many different meanings. Upon entering an Inuit home—whether in the past or today—if the woman of the household smiles, the whole world around you is just fine!

Minnie Aodla Freeman
1937–

Minnie Aodla Freeman was born on the Cape Hope Islands in James Bay in 1937. She is the granddaughter of the famous Arctic Quebec Inuit leader, Weetaltuk, who enjoyed a position of high stature in the James Bay area for half a century until his death in 1957. He navigated the boat *Laddie* that brought Robert Flaherty to Sanikiluaq (the Belcher Islands) in 1913. Minnie spent her earliest years in Moose Factory and Chisasibi (Fort-George) where she attended Anglican and Roman Catholic mission schools while also learning the traditional ways of her culture. Hospitalized with tuberculosis in Hamilton, Ontario, in 1951-1952, she used her language skills to translate for Inuit patients. At the age of sixteen, she began nurse's training at Ste. Therese School in Chisasibi, but in 1957 she moved to Ottawa to become a translator for the Department of Northern Affairs and Natural Resources.

Today an accomplished writer and gifted translator, Minnie Aodla Freeman has held a number of positions in the public media and government including serving as Assistant Editor of *Inuit Today Magazine*, as Native Cultural Advisor and Narrator for the Canadian Broadcasting Corporation, Toronto, and as Executive Secretary of the Land Claims Secretariat of the Inuit Tapirisat of Canada. She also founded and served as Manager/Producer of the Inuit Broadcasting Corporation, Ottawa, and has also held lectureships at the University of Alberta, the University of Western Ontario, Memorial University, and Arctic College. She has held consultancies with various public and private agencies and has published widely. Her writings include a book on her own life experiences, *Life Among the Qallunaat*. Minnie Aodla Freeman has been a member of the Baffin Region Writers' Group, conducting writing workshops in Iqaluit, Igloolik and Cape Dorset, and has also served as a facilitator for the International Writers Association (PEN) Eastern Arctic Tour. Her role as a facilitator and Inuktitut editor for this project has been essential to its success.

Minnie Aodla Freeman lives in Edmonton where she is married and has three children and three grandchildren.

Bibliography

"A Look at some Inuit crafts: Jewellery." Ottawa: *About Arts and Crafts* V, no. 1 (1982), pp. 3, 22, 23.

Ashevak, Kenojuak with Cynthia Cook. "Drawing Is Totally the Reverse of the Process of Carving." *Inuit Art Quarterly* 4, no. 2 (Spring 1989), pp. 23-25.

Baird, Irene. "Land of the Lively Art." *The Beaver* (Autumn 1961), pp. 12-21.

——. "Cape Dorset Man." *Canadian Geographical Journal* LXXI, no. 5 (November 1965), pp. 170-175.

Barz, Sandra, ed. *Inuit Artists Print Workbook.* 2 vols. New York: Arts and Culture of the North, 1981-1990.

Bellman, David, ed. *Peter Pitseolak (1902-1973): Inuit Historian of Seekooseelak: Photographs and Drawings from Cape Dorset, Baffin Island.* Exhibition catalogue, with essay by Dorothy Eber. Montréal: McCord Museum, 1980.

Berlo, Janet Catherine. "Inuit Women and Their Art." Exhibition brochure. St. Louis: University of Missouri St. Louis, 1988.

——. "Inuit Women and Graphic Arts: Female Creativity and Its Cultural Context." *The Canadian Journal of Native Studies* 9, no. 2 (1989), pp. 293-315.

——. "The Power of the Pencil: Inuit Women in the Graphic Arts." *Inuit Art Quarterly* 5, No. 1 (Winter 1990), pp.16-26.

——. "Pictures by Inuit: Remembering the Dismembered." Paper delivered at College Art Association of America Annual Conference, Chicago, Illinois, 1992.

Blodgett, Jean. *Eskimo Narrative.* Exhibition catalogue. Winnipeg: Winnipeg Art Gallery, 1979.

——. *Cape Dorset.* Exhibition catalogue with essays by James Houston, Alma Houston, Dorothy Eber, Terrence P. Ryan and Kananginak Pootoogook. Winnipeg: Winnipeg Art Gallery, 1979.

——. *Grasp Tight the Old Ways: Selections from the Klamer Family Collection of Inuit Art.* Exhibition catalogue. Toronto: Art Gallery of Ontario, 1983.

——. *Kenojuak.* With an essay by Patricia Ryan in collaboration with Kenojuak Ashevak, and notes by Terry Ryan. Limited edition— Toronto: Mintmark Press, 1981; Trade book— Toronto: Firefly Books, 1985.

——. *North Baffin Drawings: Collected by Terry Ryan on North Baffin Island in 1964.* Exhibition catalogue, with an essay by Terry Ryan. Toronto: Art Gallery of Ontario, 1986.

——. "Christianity and Inuit Art." *The Beaver* 315, no. 2 (Autumn 1984), pp. 16-25. Reprinted in *Inuit Art: An Anthology.* Winnipeg: Watson and Dwyer, 1988.

——. *In Cape Dorset We Do It This Way: Three Decades of Inuit Printmaking.* Exhibition catalogue with essays by Heather Ardies, Leslie Boyd and Linda Sutherland. Kleinburg: McMichael Canadian Art Collection, 1991.

Canadian Eskimo Arts Council. *Sculpture/Inuit: Sculpture of the Inuit: Masterworks of the Canadian Arctic.* Exhibition catalogue with essays by William E. Taylor, Jr., George Swinton and James Houston. Toronto: University of Toronto Press; London: Aidan Ellis Publishing, 1971.

Canadian Museum of Civilization. Unedited transcriptions of interviews with Kenojuak Ashevak, Mayoreak Ashoona, Qaunak Mikkigak, Napachie Pootoogook, Pitaloosie Saila and Ovilu Tunnillie, conducted at Cape Dorset, N.W.T., in March 1991, by Odette Leroux.

——. Unedited transcriptions of meetings with Kenojuak Ashevak, Mayoreak Ashoona, Qaunak Mikkigak, Napachie Pootoogook, Pitaloosie Saila and Ovilu Tunnillie, conducted at Cape Dorset, N.W.T., in March 1991, by Minnie Aodla Freeman and Odette Leroux.

——. Unedited transcriptions of interviews with Kenojuak Ashevak, Mayoreak Ashoona, Qaunak Mikkigak, Napachie Pootoogook, Pitaloosie Saila, Ovilu Tunnillie and Oopik Pitsiulak conducted at Cape Dorset, N.W.T., in February 1992, by Marion E. Jackson and Odette Leroux.

——, ed. *In the Shadow of the Sun: Perspective on Contemporary Native Art.* Essays on Inuit art by Dorothy Harley Eber, Helga Goetz, Ingo Hessel, Gerhard Hoffmann, Odette Leroux, Maria Muehlen, Marie Routledge, and Patricia Sutherland. Hull, Quebec: Canadian Ethnology Service, Mercury Series Paper 124, Canadian Museum of Civilization, 1993.

Collinson, Helen. *Inuit Games and Contests: The Clifford E. Lee Collection of Prints.* Exhibition catalogue. Edmonton: The University of Alberta Collections, 1978.

Craig, Mary M. "The Cape Dorset Prints." *The Beaver* (Spring 1975), pp. 22-29. Reprinted in *Inuit Art: An Anthology.* Winnipeg: Watson and Dwyer, 1988.

Crnkovich, Mary, ed. *"Gossip" A Spoken History of Women in the North.* Ottawa: Canadian Arctic Resources Committee, 1990.

Department of Indian Affairs and Northern Development, Documentation Centre, Inuit Art Section. Unedited transcriptions of interviews with Kenojuak Ashevak, Mayoreak Ashoona, Qaunak Mikkigak, Napachie Pootoogook, Pitaloosie Saila, and Ovilu Tunnillie, conducted at Cape Dorset, N.W.T., in 1979 by Marion E. Jackson.

Department of Indian and Northern Affairs, Inuit Art Section. Biographies of Cape Dorset Women Artists. 1991.

Driscoll, Bernadette. *Baffin Island.* Exhibition catalogue with essays by Lypa Pitsiulak, Gabriel Gély, and Terrence P. Ryan. Winnipeg: Winnipeg Art Gallery, 1983.

Dumas, Paul. "Gravures Esquimaudes." *Vie des arts* 18 (Spring 1960), pp. 33-37.

Eber, Dorothy Harley. *Pitseolak: Pictures out of My Life*. Edited from tape-recorded interviews by Dorothy Eber. Montréal: Design Collaborative Books in association with Oxford University Press, Toronto, 1971; Seattle: University of Washington Press, 1972.

——. "Looking for the Artists of Dorset." *The Canadian Forum* LII, no 618/619 (July/August 1972), pp. 12-16.

——. "Eskimo Penny Fashions." *North/Nord*, Vol. 20, no. 1 (January/February 1973), pp. 37-39.

——. "Johnniebo: time to set the record straight." *The Canadian Forum* 52, no. 624 (January 1973), pp. 6-9.

——. "The History of Graphics in Dorset: Long and Viable." *The Canadian Forum* 54, no. 649 (March 1975), pp. 29-31.

——. "Eskimo Tales." *Natural History* 86, no. 8 (October 1977), pp. 126-129.

——. "Visits with Pia." *The Beaver* (Winter 1983), pp. 20-27.

——. *When the Whalers Were Up North: Inuit Memories from the Eastern Arctic*. Kingston/Montréal: McGill-Queen's University Press, 1989.

Freeman, Minnie Aodla. *Life Among the Qallunaat*. Edmonton: Hurtig Publishers, 1978.

Goetz, Helga. "An Eskimo Lifetime in Pictures / Ein Eskimo-Leben in Bildern / Une vie d'Esquimau en images." *Graphis* 27, no. 157 (1972), pp. 506-512.

——. *The Inuit Print / L'estampe inuit*. Exhibition catalogue with Foreword by Willam E. Taylor, Jr. Ottawa: National Museum of Man (now the Canadian Museum of Civilization), National Museums of Canada, 1977.

Graham, K.M. "K.M. Graham's Involvement with the Cape Dorset Art Centre 1971-1977" (prepared at the request of Wallace Brannen, 3 April 1977). On file in the Documentation Centre, Inuit Art Section, Department of Indian Affairs and Northern Development.

Guemple, Lee. "Men and Women, Husbands and Wives: The Role of Gender in Traditional Inuit Society." *Études Inuit Studies* 10, nos. 1-2 (1986), pp. 9-24.

Hale, Barrie. "The Snow Prints: Inuit Visions in an Adopted Art Form." *Canadian Magazine (Toronto Star)*, 5 June 1976, pp. 8-11.

Hanson, Ann Meekitjuk. *Show Me: A young Inuk Learns How to Carve in Canada's Arctic*. Yellowknife, Northwest Territories: Amway Environmental Foundation under the auspices of the Government of the Northwest Territories and the United Nations Environment Programme, 1991.

Hoffmann, Gerhard, ed. I*m Schattten der Sonne: Zeitgenössische Kunst der Indianer und Eskimos in Kanada*. Exhibition catalogue, in German, with essays on Inuit art by Bernadette Driscoll, Dorothy Harley Eber, Helga Goetz, Ingo Hessel, Gisela Hoffmann, Odette Leroux, Maria Muehlen, Marie Routledge, and Patricia Sutherland, and entries by Angela Skinner, Dorothy Speak, and Patricia Sutherland. Stuttgart: Edition Cantz in association with the Canadian Museum of Civilization,1988.

Houston, James A. "Eskimo Graphic Art." *Canadian Art* 17, no. 1 (January 1960), pp. 8-15.

——. "Eskimo Artists." *Geographical Magazine* (London) 34, no. 11 (March 1962), pp. 639-50.

——. *Eskimo Prints*. Barre, Massachusetts: Barre, 1967; Toronto: Longman Canada, 1971.

——. "Eskimo Graphic Art: Before 1957, After 1957." *Canada Today/D'aujourd'hui* 2, no. 4 (April 1971), pp. 1-7.

Humez, Jean M. "Pictures in the Life of Eskimo Artist Pitseolak." *Woman's Art Journal* 2, no. 2 (Fall 1981/Winter 1982), pp. 30-36.

"*Inuktitut* Asks Kenojuak about Her Life as an Artist and Mother." *Inuktitut* no. 52 (January 1983), pp. 8-16.

Jackson, Marion E. "The Art of Stonecuts and Stencils: A look at the Printmaking Process." *North/Nord* 28, no.2 (Summer 1981), pp. 8-15.

——. "Personal Versus Cultural Expression in Inuit Prints." *Print Voice*, edited by Walter Jule, pp. 21-25. Edmonton: Department of Art and Design, University of Alberta, 1983.

——. "The Ashoonas of Cape Dorset: In Touch with Tradition." *North/Nord* 29, no. 3 (Fall 1983), pp. 14-18.

——. "Inuit Prints: Impressions of a Culture in Transition." *LSA* 9, no. 1 (Fall 1985), pp. 6-12.

——, and Judith M. Nasby. *Contemporary Inuit Drawings*. Exhibition catalogue. Guelph: Macdonald Stewart Art Centre, 1987.

——. *A New Day Dawning: Early Cape Dorset Prints*. Ann Arbor, Michigan: University of Michagan Museum of Art, 1989.

Kahn, Charles, and Maureen Kahn. *Canadians All: 3 Portraits of Our People*. Toronto: Methuen Publications, 1979.

Labarge, Dorothy. "Femme traditionnelle, femme nouvelle." *North/Nord* 22, no. 5. (October 1975), pp. 8-11.

——. "Cape Dorset Engravings." Exhibition brochure with text by Alex Wyse. Ottawa: Department of Indian Affairs and Northern Development, 1978.

——. *From Drawing to Print: Perception and Process in Cape Dorset Art*. Exhibition catalogue. Calgary: Glenbow Museum, 1986.

Lipton, Barbara. *Arctic Vision: Art of the Canadian Inuit*. Exhibition catalogue. Ottawa: Canadian Arctic Producers, 1984.

National Gallery of Canada. *Cape Dorset: A Decade of Eskimo Prints and Recent Sculptures*. Ottawa: National Gallery of Canada, National Museums of Canada, 1967.

National Museum of Man (now Canadian Museum of Civilization). "The Cape Dorset Print: Commemorating Twenty-five Years of Printmaking at Cape Dorset." Exhibition brochure for an exhibition held at Rideau Hall. Ottawa: National Museum of Man, National Museums of Canada, 1983.

Opperman, Hal. "The Inuit Phenomenon in Art – Historical Context." *Inuit Art Quarterly* 1, no. 2 (Summer 1986), pp. 1-4.

Patterson, Nancy-Lou, and Erla Socha. "Recent Trends in Canadian Native Printmaking." *Artmagazine* 8, no. 31/32 (March/April 1977), pp. 48-53.

Pitseolak. *Pitseolak*. Cape Dorset, N.W.T.: West Baffin Eskimo Co-operative, in co-operation with the Department of Indian and Northern Affairs, [n.d.].

Pitseolak, Peter and Dorothy Harley Eber. *People from our Side: a Life Story with Photographs and Oral Biography*. Edmonton: Hurtig Publishers, 1975 and Montréal: McGill-Queen's University Press, 1993.

Pratt, Mary. "Art of the Caribou People." *The Denver Magazine* 6, no. 9 (August 1970), pp. 36-40.

Reeves, John. "The Women Artists of Cape Dorset." *City and Country Home* (April 1985), pp. 35-43.

Ritchie, Carson I.A. *The Eskimo and His Art*. Toronto: The Macmilllan Company of Canada, 1974. (London and New York, 1975)

Robertson, John K. "Carvings and Prints by the Family of Pitseolak." Gallery brochure. Ottawa: Robertson Galleries, 1967.

Roch, Ernst, ed. *Arts of the Eskimo: Prints*. Montréal: Signum Press in association with Oxford University Press, 1974.

Routledge, Marie. *Inuit Art in the 1970s*. Exhibition catalogue. Kingston: Agnes Etherington Art Centre, [n.d.].

——. with Marion E. Jackson. *Pudlo: Thirty Years of Drawing*. Exhibition catalogue. Ottawa: National Gallery of Canada, 1990.

Saila, Pitaloosie. "Pitaloosie Saila Talks about Old Age, Her First Drawing, White People and Other Things." *Inuit Art Quarterly* 2, no. 3 (Summer 1987), pp. 10-12.

Stevenson, A. "Then Came the Traders." *Inuit Women in Transition*. Ottawa: Department of Indian and Northern Affairs, 1975.

Swinton, George. *Sculpture of the Eskimo*. Toronto: McClelland and Stewart, 1972. Rev. ed. *Sculpture of the Inuit*. Toronto: McClelland and Stewart, 1992.

Swinton. Nelda. *The Inuit Sea Goddess/La Déesse [inuit] inuite de la mer*. Exhibition catalogue. Montréal: Montréal Museum of Fine Arts, 1980.

Van Raalte, Sharon. "Inuit Women and Their Art." *Communiqué* (May 1975), pp. 21-23.

Vastokas, Joan M. "Continuities in Eskimo Graphic Syle." *Artscanada* 27, no. 6 (December 1971-January 1972), pp. 69-83.

Watt, Virginia J., ed. *The Permanent Collection: Inuit Arts and Crafts, c. 1900-1980*. Catalogue with essays by Virginia J. Watt, Helga Goetz and Marybelle Myers. Montréal: Canadian Guild of Crafts Quebec, 1980.

West Baffin Eskimo Co-operative Ltd. Annual graphics collection catalogues, 1959-1994.

Winnipeg Art Gallery. *Cape Dorset: Selected Sculpture from the Collection of the Winnipeg Art Gallery*. Exhibition catalogue. Winnipeg: Winnipeg Art Gallery, 1975.

Withers, Josephine. "Inuit Women Artists: An Art Essay." *Feminist Studies* 10, no. 1 (Spring 1984), pp. 84-96.

Witt, Bert. "The Eskimo Woman: Her Life and Dreams in Prints and Sculpture." Gallery brochure. Los Angeles: The Arctic Circle, 1977.